Demystifying Deleuze

An Introductory Assemblage of Crucial Concepts

Edited by:
Rob Shields and Mickey Vallee

© Red Quill Books Ltd. 2012
Ottawa

www.redquillbooks.com
ISBN 978-1-926958-20-0

Printed on acid-free paper. The paper used in this book incorporates post-consumer waste and has not been sourced from endangered old growth forests, forests of exceptional conservation value or the Amazon Basin. Red Quill Books subscribes to a one-book-at-a-time manufacturing process that substantially lessens supply chain waste, reduces greenhouse emissions, and conserves valuable natural resources.

Library and Archives Canada Cataloguing in Publication

Demystifying Deleuze : an assemblage of crucial concepts / edited by Rob Shields and Mickey Vallee.

Includes bibliographical references.
ISBN 978-1-926958-20-0

1. Deleuze, Gilles. I. Shields, Rob, 1961- II. Vallee, Mickey, 1976- III. Title.
B2430.D454D46 2013   194   C2012-906916-7

[RQB is a radical publishing house.
Part of the proceeds from the sale of this book will support student scholarships.]

Introduction 7 Actualization 11
Affects 13 Animal/Becoming-Animal 17 Arboroscent (compare Rhizomatic) 21 Art and Creativity 25
Assemblage 29 Becoming 33
Body without Organs (BwO) 37
Control/Societies of Control 41
Desire 47 Difference 51
Duration 53 Ecosophy 55
Emergence 59 Event 61
Fabulation 65 Faciality 67 Flow 69
Fold 71 Force 75 Haecceities 79
Image of Thought 83 Immanence / Plane of Immanence 87 Imperceptible (Becoming) 91 Intensity/Intensive 95
Line, Line of Flight 99
Machine 103

Machinic Assemblage 107
Majoritarian/Minoritarian 111
Minor 113   Molar/Molecular 117
Multiplicity 121   Nomadic 125
Percepts 129
Plane of Composition 133
Plane of Consistency 137
Potential 141   Power 145
Refrain 149   Rhizome/Arborescent 153
Schizoanalysis 157   Sense 161
Smooth Space 163   Strata 167
Striated Space 171   Subject 175
Subjectification 179   Time Image/
Action Image 183   Virtual/Actual 189
War Machine 195   Contributors 199

DEMYSTIFYING DELEUZE

Introduction
The wasp and the orchid

For our students, families and friends.

Demystifying Deleuze is more than a guide to the basic theoretical edifice of Gilles Deleuze. It is a workbook. It puts concepts into motion rather than clarifying them for comprehension; it builds tools for use instead of identifying names to remember; it primes the reader for working through difficult pages of original text instead of standing in to make the concepts appear autonomous. And although Deleuze's long time writing partner, Félix Guattari, is absent in the title of this book, his work and influence is pervasive in the entries which follow. Without question, he deserves a workbook of his own.

Demystifying Deleuze will tell you nothing of his life. The entries are stand-alone and about as straightforward as we could hope. Each entry provides Deleuze (and Guattari's) description of a key idea, strategic quotations that are now found throughout discussions of their work, and sense of how the idea has developed. Rather than closing down debate as a definition would, the entries conclude with further reading and a sense of the puzzle or the debate that each idea continues to provoke. We *want* Deleuzean thought to be accessible, yet we equally want the reader to understand that the knots of his thought cannot simply be undone. The concepts shouldn't make the reader contemplate. They should rouse and mobilize the reader to their own concepts that render the world in fresh new ways.

There are pragmatic aspects to this book. It is, certainly, written primarily as a reference tool for students and scholars and interested readers. But the entries are more than explanations for surviving a course or a literature review or a dinner conversation. They are made with the intention of welcoming the reader to the possibility of working through the distinctive mode Deleuze uses to generate concepts. Like the wasp and the orchid, so are the book and the reader: "Wasp and orchid, as heterogeneous elements, form a rhizome", Deleuze and Guattari explain in *A Thousand Plateaus*, which is "not imitation at all but a capture of code, surplus value of code, an increase in valence, a veritable becoming, a becoming-wasp of the orchid and a becoming-orchid of the wasp." The book should engage you in a process of not only becoming fascinated with Deleuze's thought but by what you might do with it.

If the social sciences and humanities are bound by a common concern, we think it is in the pursuit of conditions that produce change: any reconceptualization that accounts for the creation of something new. Our aim is to be concise without sacrificing the complex nuances of Deleuzean thought so that the reader can use the book as a passage towards reconceptualization. At the same time, however, if this book grounds Deleuzean thought for the reader, it should be remembered that the ground cannot identify with what it grounds, since it is difference which produces the two, and ultimately difference which produces the new. Get on with your own understanding and practice.

Rob Shields and Mickey Vallee

Rob Shields is the author of many books. He holds the Henry Marshall Tory Endowed Research Chair in Sociology and Art and Design at University of Alberta where he facilitates participatory public research. He is a theorist of cities, social space, and the intangibility of culture.

Mickey Vallee is an assistant professor of sociology at the University of Lethbridge, where he specializes in psychoanalytic cultural theory, poststructural philosophy, popular culture, and the sociology of music.

DEMYSTIFYING DELEUZE

Actualization
Mickey Vallee

Actualization is the coming forth of the virtual into the actual. In *Difference & Repetition*, Deleuze (1994) prefers the term *actualization* to representation, because the latter relies on a binary system of thought he critiqued throughout his career (pp. 233-234, 255-256, 258-259, 261-262, 306-307). Actualization is related to expression, stemming from his persistent interest in the world as itself an expressive and immanent entity. The world consists of neither representations, nor is it directly inhabited without mediation.

In *A Thousand Plateaus* (2004), Deleuze and Guattari define actualization as occurring specifically in the plane of immanence (pp. 170-176). The plane of immanence is constituted at the interface of the virtual and its actualization, which is simultaneously the point at which the actual object folds back into the virtual images that support it.

Every experienced moment that presents itself as an actualization is brought to a plane by moments of the past, and its significance folds back into the virtual structure of the past which sustains it. As Todd May writes, "There is no present that does not actualize the past. It is all of the past that is actualized at every moment. The past that is actualized exists" (2005, p. 52). Actualization is the past as it is lived throughout an unfolding present that folds back into the past. There are no cuts with Deleuze, as if the present is cut from the past, only ongoing continuities, flows, and unfoldings. Memories are a fold in this virtual fabric: "degrees or modes of actualization which are spread out between two extremes of the actual and the virtual: the actual and its virtual on the small circuit, expanding virtualities in the deep circuits" (Deleuze, 2005, p. 78).

Reality, for Deleuze, is always virtual-actual (a virtuality gives birth to its own actualization). The virtual and the actual are entwined in one another.

References

Deleuze, Gilles. *Difference and Repetition.* New York: Columbia University Press, 1994.

Deleuze, Gilles. *Cinema 2: The Time Image.* London: Continuum, 2005.

Deleuze, Gilles and Felix Guattari. *A Thousand Plateaus: Capitalism and Schizophrenia.* London: Continuum, 2004.

May, Todd. *Gilles Deleuze: An Introduction.* Cambridge University Press, 2005.

Affects
Matthew Tiessen

Deleuze follows Spinoza (a seventeenth-century rationalist philosopher who opposed Descartes' Cartesian maxim, "I think hence I exist") in defining affects as, simply, forces that things exert upon other things. These forces, in turn, become actualized so long as they find a purchase on those other things. They are known through their effects. Deleuze imagines that their requirements (their "desires," so to speak) are satisfied and enabled by their environment and context. For Deleuze, affect spoke of the non-representational mode of thought (see becoming).

Spinoza discovered that individuals are defined solely by their relations, and that these relations are always changing. This means individuals are changing. For Spinoza, the world is immanent and full of potential (see immanence). It is defined by forces that affect and are affected. Affective exchanges are not predictable. The constituents that participate in these exchanges are always being affected differently. How can we predict what will happen in a minute, when the present is redefining the terms of the question?

In the subsequent literature, Massumi (2002) demonstrates that affect pervades - indeed, inaugurates - our experience of the emotional and rational, the cognitive and physical moments of our lives. Affect, understood here in the Spinozist sense, is distributed through an interchange of cause and effect: one thing can affect another, or another can affect it. In other words, an affect does not exist on its own, but - like any quality - comes into existence only in the presence of something that can be affected. The affects that constitute the affectability of things are relational - affects are relation's effects. Deleuze's ontology emphasizes the significance of this affective interchange. Affect's significance, for Deleuze and for us here, rests in the observation that everything derives its existence from the give and take that it enables, for it is only within an economy of give and take, of cause and effect, of comparison and contrasts, that meaning, materiality, or any other actualization comes into being. Or, as Deleuze might say, in order for force to exist, it must be pre-existed by exertion and resistance; indeed, force itself can be understood not as a thing, but instead as the effect of two entities in relation to one another (of course, these entities not only exert force, but are defined by the force - that which exists in between actor and acted-upon - they exert):

> *A body which moves* or *is at rest must be determined to motion or rest by another body, which has also been determined to motion or rest by another, and that again by another, and so on, to infinity.* [...] Cor.: From this it follows that a body in motion moves until it is determined by another body to rest; and that a body at rest also remains at rest until it is determined to motion by another. [...] All modes by which a body is affected by another body follow both from the nature of the body affected and at the same time from the nature of the affecting body, so that one and the same body may be moved differently according to differences in the nature of the bodies moving it. And conversely, different bodies may be moved differently by one and the same body. (Spinoza, 1996, pp. 40-41)

In Deleuze and Guattari's view, affective experience constitutes a form of thinking equal (but different) to that performed by philosophy. Affects, in their view, define any organism:

> We know nothing about a body until we know what it can do, in other words, what its affects are, how they can or cannot enter into composition with other affects, with the affects of another body, either to destroy that body or be destroyed by it, either to exchange actions and passions with it or to join with it in composing a more powerful body (Deleuze and Guattari, 2004, p. 284).

As Massumi observes: "Expression is always fundamentally of a relation, not of a subject. In the expression, process and product are one" (Massumi, 2002, p. xxiv). Affect and affect's manipulation is, for Deleuze, an important topic to grapple with when we want to think about how becoming takes place, whether aesthetic, linguistic, scientific, or biological. Deleuze regards affect as prelinguistic, as the original enabler of all that follows, of all instances of being affected. For Deleuze, affect precedes language and is language's precondition. Massumi suggests that Deleuze and Guattari would argue that we do not speak so much as we are spoken through or with; that is, the subject is "in a sense spoken by extra-linguistic [i.e. affective] forces of expression, and that this impersonal speaking is not a matter of choice" (p. xvii). The "force of expression," Massumi observes, "strikes the body first, directly and unmediatedly"; from there it passes "transformatively through the flesh before being instantiated in subject-positions subsumed by a system of power. Its immediate effect is a differing" (p. xvii). Alan Bourassa (in Massumi, 2002, p. 65) observes that Deleuze's affect describes anything that "comes into being when something is affected or affects something else" and that affect is "the determination (which must always be actual) that founds all potentiality." Language, Bourassa notes, is always "filled with affects" and would, as noted here, "have no existence without them" (p. 65).

References

Deleuze, Gilles and Felix Guattari. *A Thousand Plateaus: Capitalism and Schizophrenia.* London: Continuum, 2004.

Massumi, Brian. *A Shock to Thought: Expression After Deleuze and Guattari.* New York: Routledge, 2002.

Spinoza, Benedict de. *Ethics.* London: Penguin Books, 1996.

Animal/ Becoming- Animal

Jason Wallin

Deleuze's animal is distinguished from the image of a domesticated animal or a pet. For Deleuze, the domestic farm animal is already too familiar insofar as it drawn into a psychoanalytically informed Oedipal image of the family through which its difference and wildness is nullified.

Deleuze points to this nullification in classical psychoanalysis, wherein animal imagery and encounters are often projected onto the image of the human family. Such a scene of domestication is exemplified in *A Thousand Plateaus* (2004a), where Deleuze and Guattari recount Freud's clinical interpretation that his patient's dream of a wolf pack represents the primordial father. Against such domesticating interpretation machines (a condemning term for psychoanalysis), Deleuze and Guattari argue that when a person enters into a relationship with an animal, this relationship can no longer be thought of in strictly human terms. Yet, the human-animal relationship has nothing to do with imitating animals. Rather, it is a relationship composed by emitting molecules (impalpable dynamics) that enter into composition with those of the animal (pp. 29-43).

For instance, in the 1976 movie *Taxi Driver*, when Robert De Niro walks like a crab (he considered the character he played, Travis Bickle, to be particularly indirect, hence to move from side to side like a crab), he is not attempting to imitate an actual crab, but rather seeks to draw something particular to the crab into composition with the image of "crab-ness" (Deleuze and Guattari, 2004a, p. 303). This is to say that animal-becomings do not take place at the level of representation or resemblance (what Deleuze calls the "molar" level, see also actualization). As with all becoming, becoming-animal is thus always molecular. More specifically, becoming-animal is a question of how one might create a zone of intensity with an animal, or rather, in proper Deleuzean terminology, a body without organs that enters into composition with animal intensities. For Deleuze (2005), such an experiment is exemplified in the artwork of Francis

Bacon, where the deformation of human heads composes a zone of indiscernability that palpates an inhuman experience in the body. For Deleuze and Guattari (2004a), becoming-animal is an assemblage or unnatural union that mobilizes difference in what might otherwise be a programmed or overdetermined image of the body (p. 302).

In *What is Philosophy?* (1994), Deleuze and Guattari assert that the territorializing behaviours of particular animals mark the origins of art in its purest state. What is of interest to Deleuze and Guattari are the ways in which the animal composes a territory through posture, colour and song. Even when certain animals depart from their territories, they create vectors of reterritorialization elsewhere (see refrain). It is in this way that the behaviours of particular animals serve as a precursor to Deleuze and Guattari's philosophical conceptualization of territorialization, deterritorialization, and reterrritorialization. The animal creates a world by emitting and reacting to signs. For example, a bird's song produces a territory from the decoded body of the earth. The bird sings, and this sound establishes the bird's territory as an acoustic effect for all in hearing range. For such animals as the tick, a world of signs and affects can be extremely limited (pp. 183-187).

For example, Deleuze and Gauttari (2004a) refer to the world of the tick in terms of only three affects: sensitivity to light, the smell of mammals, and of burrowing at the point of easiest access. This is, in part, what it means for the writer, the artist or philosopher to become-animal. Yet, this definition of the animal must be connected to Deleuze's conceptualization of the animal's world insofar as the writer, the artist, or philosopher must first compose a territory through the emission of signs. In this vein, Deleuze suggests that the becoming-animal of the philosopher, the writer or artist is linked to the creation of a unique syntax, or rather, a style of thinking in place of the animal. Deleuze and Guattari detect such a becoming-animal in the works of Kafka, Joyce and Carroll, wherein an original world is created through the emission and sensitive reception of unique signs (Deleuze and Guattari, 1986).

Becoming-animal has nothing to do with imitation of animals, but rather, the formation of alliances with fringe or secret groups at the edge of centralizing institutions. In this vein, becoming-animal is always a profoundly creative movement of registering a world, a practice or a style of thought that no longer falls back upon an anthropocentric image of the family or State, producing instead an inhuman or other-than-human composition capable of creating new forms of expression for living (Deleuze and Guattari, 2004b).

References

Deleuze, Gilles. *Francis Bacon: The Logic of Sensation*. London: Continuum, 2005.

Deleuze, Gilles and Felix Guattari. *A Thousand Plateaus: Capitalism and Schizophrenia*. London: Continuum, 2004a.

Deleuze, Gilles and Felix Guattari. *Anti-Oedipus: Capitalism and Schizophrenia*. London: Continuum, 2004b.

Deleuze, Gilles and Felix Guattari. *Kafka: Toward a Minor Literature*. Minneapolis: University of Minnesota Press, 1986.

Deleuze, Gilles and Felix Guattari. *What Is Philosophy?* New York: Columbia University Press, 1994.

Arboroscent (compare Rhizomatic)

Bradley
Lafortune

In a word, the arborescent is any schema that, in advance of critical examination, "holds things together" (Deleuze and Guattari, 1987, p. 327). In general, the category of the "arborescent" has an unmistakably negative connotation in Deleuze and Guattari's philosophy.

For Deleuze and Guattari, "arborescent" is an inclusive and fundamental category encapsulating the dominant characteristics and primary objects of their critique: linearity, hierarchy, territoriality, molarity, centrality, identity, systems of judgment (i.e. morality), stasis, and, the apotheosis of their critique, the supposed metaphysical consistency of "being." As iconoclasts, it is no wonder that Deleuze and Guattari have little patience for such organizing schemas; indeed, they are "tired of trees" for "they've made us suffer too much" (1987, p. 15).

The negativity of the figure of the arborescent (i.e. tree-like) is not due to its symbolic significance as a figure for life or growth, but rather for its structural significance as a figure for order, individuality and organization. The arborescent represents the opposite of the potentiality of "becoming(s)" (see Deleuze and Guattari, 1987, Chapter 10). The arborescent insists upon "centers of significance and subjectification" (p. 16); *becoming(s) allow for de-centered and de-subjectified proliferations of flows, forces and desires.*

The "arborescent" becomes most clear in contrast to another conceptual category: the "rhizomatic." Whereas "a rhizome has no beginning or end" and "is always in the middle," remaining in a constant state of becoming (Deleuze and Guattari, 1987, p. 25), the arborescent implies origins or ends and ontological stasis, remaining in a stagnant state of being. Yet Deleuze and Guattari are quick to recall that, despite the desire for a simple and instructive binary system, "there are knots of arborescence in rhizomes, and rhizomatic offshoots in roots" (p. 20), challenging the notion that, through these metaphors, one could arrive at a final model for an ethics of thought. Indeed, the contrast between the arborescent and rhizomatic "is not a new or different dualism" as

ARBOROSCENT (COMPARE RHIZOMATIC)

a diametrical opposition, but the employment of a dualistic model "in order to arrive at a process that challenges all models" (p. 20).

Since the fundamental task for thought in philosophy is "creating concepts" (Deleuze and Guattari, 1994, p. 5), all hierarchical and static arborescent schemas that shut down the potential for creative interactions between thought, concepts, ideas, people and disciplines - what Deleuze calls "the powers of life" in *Cinema I* and *Cinema II* (1986; 1989) - are contrary to the possibility of the creation of the new. Closing down the possibility of new forms of knowledge in advance, the arborescent diminishes vitality, creativity and desire, and as such, functions as the fundamental category that a philosophy worthy of the name must resist through the creative proliferations of and experimentations with multiplicities, becoming(s) and rhizomes. Defining the arborescent and identifying its forms (the State and the Oedipalized family come to mind immediately) is a primary task for a philosophical and ethical project that considers vitality, creativity, desire and thought to be of the highest importance. Subsequently, dismantling the arborescent is part of the larger project of maintaining the future possibilities of philosophy and thought - possibilities that extend far beyond the specific disciplinary domain of philosophy and reach into the ethical territory of the creative powers of life itself.

References

Deleuze, Gilles. *Cinema 1: The Movement Image.* Minneapolis: University of Minnesota Press, 1986.

Deleuze, Gilles. *Cinema 2: The Time Image.* Minneapolis: University of Minnesota Press, 1989.

Deleuze, Gilles and Felix Guattari. *A Thousand Plateaus: Capitalism and Schizophrenia.* Minneapolis: University of Minnesota Press, 1987.

Deleuze, Gilles and Felix Guattari. *What Is Philosophy?* New York: Columbia University Press, 1994.

Art and Creativity
M. Tiessen

Deleuze sets "art" apart from philosophy or science by way of its emphasis on affect (not necessarily feeling). In Deleuzean terms, art's fundamental mode of operation is the *actualization of affects*. A work of art is, Deleuze and Guattari suggest in *What Is Philosophy?* (1994), "a bloc of sensations" or "a compound of percepts and affects" (p. 164). Deleuze and Guattari (1994) contend that art "thinks no less than philosophy," but art that "thinks" differently "through affects and percepts rather than through concepts (p. 66). Deleuze argues that despite their being distinct, art and philosophy are intertwined, and at times, can be indistinguishable, for while their mediums might be different, good art and good philosophy - those that avoid clichés - are both in pursuit of the new: art through the use of affect, philosophy through the use of concepts.

The Deleuzean approach to art sees it as an activity that responds to investigations into the unseen and unforeseen, revealing the limitation of vision. Similarly, the production of art reveals to the artist the inadequacy of imagination (since one can only imagine that which already exists within the confines of one's mind). To produce art *is* thus to produce the new itself, that which the observer was unable to see before interrogating the unseen.

Artists seek out un(fore)seen affects, and once these affects are discovered - once something is revealed to be *more* or *newly* affecting - artists harness these affects using paint, print, stone, light, sound, touch and so on. But artists do not just create affects "in their work," write Deleuze and Guattari (1994), they "give them to us," making us become "with them" – we get drawn "into the compound" (p. 175). Art speaks the language of sensation, of affect: "Whether through words, colors, sounds, or stone, art is the language of sensations" (p. 176).

Art thus fits under the Deleuzean scheme of non-representational affect (see actualization). It reserves judgment (so to speak), instead being open to the interpretation of others, to the proliferation of what it produces: affect. So called non-representational painting is not "abstract" for Deleuze and Guattari; rather, *all* art is abstract insofar as it seeks the unknown, summons "forces" in order to exhibit them using canvas, paint and wood (see molecular assemblages). The affects produced by painting never remain within the painting's frame and instead circulate freely amidst spectators' bodies, mingling with the forces inherent to other works, being impacted by critics, times, places, etc. (see action-image).

In the face of art-making's Dionysian expressions, there is always some sort of structure upon which, or into which, the art is created. At the very least, art always has a site, a location (even if its more virtual/atmospheric/ephemeral manifestations find their location or have their effects on our bodies). For example, even Jackson Pollock's paintings - free marks in their entirety - are captured and restrained by the canvas (although his paint splashing undoubtedly exceeded the boundaries of the canvas during the painting's production). There is, then, always a scaffolding, a framing, an imposed order, a context, a scene, a time/space into which the art is inserted. Deleuze and Guattari (1994) warn us that even as we pursue lines of flight and hysteria through the creation of, for example, free marks, we (i.e. we as a bundle of affects, as composite compositions) risk implosion, self-destruction, if we fly out of control: "We require just a little order to protect us from chaos" (p. 202).

References

Deleuze, Gilles and Felix Guattari. *What Is Philosophy?* New York: Columbia University Press, 1994.

DEMYSTIFYING DELEUZE

Assemblage
Erin Kruger

Assemblage is defined by Deleuze and Guattari (1987) as a process of positioning multiple and heterogeneous elements in the service of establishing a territory. It is the mix of contingency and organization, such as the chance subcultural expressions that come from contingent historical/economic conditions which in turn express the strata of a particular social group (mods in London in the 1960s, for instance). Defined by their ability to coalesce singularities as they emerge from flows, assemblages congeal into constellations through the convergence and stratification of any possible number of traits, but their dominant characteristics remain those of malleability. Thus, synergies are productive in the sense that they gather any number of "things" (i.e. pieces or particles, moleculars) into a singular context, forging new meanings and possibilities.

Assemblages are composed of a vertical axis that deals with signs and symbols, and a horizontal axis dealing with its machinic elements. The horizontal axis is where the break-up and transformations of input flows (segments) responds to physical systems and combines organs and machines into organized "bodies." These bodies can be human and inhuman (e.g. that of a person, or of a body-politic).

Deleuze and Guattari point to the example of subjectivity as a means of elucidating the new in the assemblage. The subject is a long-standing point of contention for Deleuze and Guattari. In opposition to philosophers of consciousness, they maintain it is not a singular body that defines subjectivity, but a composition put together from pieces and prior collections. For example, the subject is differentiated from the biological body in that the latter is composed of organs, membranes, nerves, physio-chemical processes, all the while sustained through the tools the body requires: nourishment, shelter, transport, love. The subject is therefore not a static or unified entity, but an "imposed web of connections and codes, flows of energy, segments and strata," whose coordinates are contingently related to the biological and organic human body (Bogard, 1998, pp. 52-7). Moreover, producing the subject is never consistent and often occurs through disrupting bodies and juxtaposing bodily parts to form new social orders.

For Deleuze and Guattari (1987), the social, political and ethical significance of the assemblage is the inherent multiplicity and contingency that defines and produces transformative systems without definitive meanings or organizations. Pragmatically, this conceptual openness makes the assemblage an excellent tool for sociological theorizing and analysis. The assemblage can formulate a collective from what otherwise appears to be disparate elements and thus forges connections from diverse and numerous orders. The territorial nature of the assemblage allows it to temporarily "settle" into a coherent and stable formation, while the deterritorialized capacity enables the subsequent destabilization of this system, allowing it to be "carried away" (p. 88). Together, the interaction of these forces creates assemblages that are characterized by forms of expression and signifying regimes all of which correspond to the continual interchange of formations and destabilization.

References

Bogard, William. "Sense and Segmentarity: Some Markers of a Deleuzeian-Guattarian Sociology." *Sociological Theory*, Vol. 16, No. 1, (March 1998), pp. 52-74.

Deleuze, Gilles and Felix Guattari. *A Thousand Plateaus: Capitalism and Schizophrenia*. Minneapolis: University of Minnesota Press, 1987.

DEMYSTIFYING DELEUZE

Becoming
M. Tiessen

Deleuze's concept of becoming is aligned closely, if not an illustrative example of, Spinoza's philosophy of affect (*affectus* = affect, *affectio* = affection), a non-representational mode of thought. Affect, Spinoza elaborates in Part III of his *Ethics*, describes the effects of relations between bodies, or in proper Deleuzean terms, processes of entities' affecting and being affected through emergent processes of inter-relational becoming. In his lecture on Spinoza, Deleuze describes this process in a simple example:

> I feel the affection of the sun on me, the trace of the sun on me. It's the effect of the sun on my body. But the causes, that is, that which is my body, that which is the body of the sun, and the relation between these two bodies such that the one produces a particular effect on the other rather than something else, of these things I know [*sais*] absolutely nothing. (Deleuze and Guattari, 1987, p. 256)

In a further elaboration of this Spinozian line, Deleuze and Guattari explain that these "[a]ffects are becomings. Spinoza asks: What can a body do? We call the latitude of a body the affects of which it is capable at a given degree of power, or rather within the limits of that degree" (p. 256).

Deleuze, in following Nietzsche, conceives of the world as less a collective of representations and more a series of productions, expressions, and assemblages - each quality is adequately real, unique, and expressive of difference. Deleuze regards any worldview that perpetuates the ideology of transcendental philosophy (i.e. one which evaluates and assesses the merits of this world against another more perfect one) ultimately impoverishes the creative and immanent processes of life.

Deleuze's use of the concept "becoming" reflects his long-standing emphasis on reality itself as a perpetual process of becoming, of ongoing repetitions of difference. Becoming, for Deleuze and Guattari, does not "happen" (as in the degree to which a significant event "happens") because it is always in the process of happening (of becoming). As they explain in *What is Philosophy?* (1994), "Without history, becoming would remain indeterminate and unconditioned, but becoming is not historical. Psychosocial types belong to history, but conceptual personae belong to becoming. The event itself needs becoming as an unhistorical element" (96). This notion that events need becoming, and that becoming itself must be thought of as "unhistorical," implies that events are conditioned by transhistorical becoming, since becoming is what everything is doing all the time. As the title of Deleuze's book *Difference and Repetition* (1994) suggests, the only constant in our world - the only thing that is forever repeated - is difference, or processes of differentiation. In other words, perpetual differentiation is an expression of ongoing processes of becoming different.

References

Deleuze, Gilles. *Difference and Repetition.* New York: Columbia University Press, 1994.

Deleuze, Gilles and Felix Guattari. *A Thousand Plateaus: Capitalism and Schizophrenia.* Minneapolis: University of Minnesota Press, 1987.

Deleuze, Gilles and Felix Guattari. *What Is Philosophy?* New York: Columbia University Press, 1994.

DEMYSTIFYING DELEUZE

Body without Organs (BwO)

Jason Wallin

The Body without Organs is a body without organization. It is the body (human or otherwise, such as a body of water or a body of work) removed from the habits of social and individual ordering. While the term Body without Organs (BwO) is drawn from Antonin Artaud's (1975) radio play *To Have Done With The Judgment of God*, in the Deleuzean context, it is more adequately understood in relation to the work of Karl Marx (in *Anti-Oedipus*) and Melanie Klein (in *A Thousand Plateaus*, 2004a. In *Anti-Oedipus* (2004b), the BwO constitutes a diagram for the surplus power of capital, which deterritorializes social and economic machines in contradistinction to the regimented society of the feudal period. Capitalism's forms of accumulation require the dissolution of relations of production (the feudal subject's bond to the soil and guild, for example) in an effort to "free" stratified labor to contribute to the fluid body of capital (the BwO). As Deleuze and Guattari demonstrate, the reorganization of "social organs" (objects) in relation to capital functions parasitically upon the laborer (since the power of the worker becomes attributed to capital), in turn making capital appear as a "natural or divine presupposition" (pp. 12-13).

Insofar as the BwO functions as a power of connection for binding social and subjective organs (objects) to capital, it overlaps with disjunctive processes in which the subject or individuated body is differentiated from the smooth, or decoded, surface of labour. Related to the somatic rupture of repression, the body becomes, through psychoanalysis, an ordered site of control under the careful gaze of the expert. For example, someone's mannerisms or ticks take on an arrangement, a logic connected to the truth regime of the expert.

Later, in its more familiar deployment in *A Thousand Plateaus* (2004a), Deleuze and Guattari redeploy the BwO as a force of deterritorialization. Drawing from the underdeveloped notion of the liquid or urethral object in Klein's object-relation

BODY WITHOUT ORGANS (BWO)

theory, Deleuze and Guattari ask how the body is composed in the first place, advancing the BwO as the experimental practices that remake a body that is always actual-virtual. Referencing Spinoza's *Ethics* as the "Great Book of the BwO" (p. 170), Deleuze and Guattari assert that we do not yet know what a body can do (see affect). Of specific concern here is the overdetermination of the body via the dogmatic arrangement of its organs. Railing against the *a priori* mapping of bodily intensities (drives) presupposed by classical psychoanalysis, priestly authority and governmentality, Deleuze and Guattari advance the BwO as the "field of immanence of desire" (p. 173). Put differently, the BwO is the immanent, undifferentiated plane of energy in and through which all-desiring production becomes possible (both virtual and actual).

Depending on the kinds of intensities one seeks to palpate, the BwO might be composed in different ways. The BwO of a junkie (who aspires to palpate what Deleuze and Guattari dub refrigeration waves) is different than that of the masochist (who produces a BwO that attempts to palpate pain waves) (1987, p. 170). Deleuze and Guattari articulate three instances of the BwO: the cancerous, the empty, and the full. The cancerous BwO fails as an experiment insofar as it becomes caught in routine patterns and habits of production. Brought about by the absolute deterritorialization of flows and intensities, the empty BwO leads to a kind of catatonia. With the full BwO, Deleuze and Guattari advance a productive image of experimentation that avoids becoming over-organized in its cautious approach to deterritorialization.

You never realize, or more properly, actualize the BwO; it is always out of reach. It is an image without likeness; it resists organization. It is the anarchist body, denaturalized.

References

Artaud, Antonin. *To Have Done With The Judgment Of God*. Boston: Black Sparrow Press, 1975.

Deleuze, Gilles and Felix Guattari. *A Thousand Plateaus: Capitalism and Schizophrenia*. London: Continuum, 2004a.

Deleuze, Gilles and Felix Guattari. *Anti-Oedipus: Capitalism and Schizophrenia*. London: Continuum, 2004b.

Control/ Societies of Control

Ronjon Paul Datta

Deleuze elaborates his concept of control in "Postscript on Control Societies" (1995) in which he offers a diagnosis of post-WWII Western societies. Control is about regulating, modulating and channeling flows, frequently regulating people's access and movement via passwords/codes (especially as concerns access to information). For example, access and traffic to databases is controlled by regulating who gets a password. Or, more along the lines of Deleuze's preference for hydraulic models, another kind of control is that found on a home-heating thermostat with hot-water/radiator heating. In this case, a thermostat controls how open or closed valves are, thus regulating the flow of hot water through pipes to the radiator in a room, in turn allowing one to control the temperature. Deleuze suggests that power in contemporary Western societies functions according to the same logic of control.

Control amounts to a "new system [or type] of domination" (1995, p. 182) dependent on a distinct way of organizing power. Control is contemporaneous with the spread of: computerization; digitalization; dependence on informational inputs; and a global capitalist division of labour. Contemporary capitalism is a major condition of the emergence of societies of control in the West. Production is increasingly carried out in the East and Third World, and the "metaproduction" (1995, p. 181) of marketing, servicing and sales of products made in the East happens in the West. Capitalist control in the West thus channels production and exchanges across the globe. Free-floating currency exchange rates are also an example of control, since what regulates the prices of currencies are the flows of the currencies traded around the world everyday, thereby facilitating modulations of production and metaproduction.

Domination in control societies is quite different from using direct physical force or laws on individuals and groups. Instead of passing laws forbidding certain behaviours, people are "re-routed." For example, instead of making political protest illegal or making it likely that there will be a confrontation between protesters and riot police, police route and re-route the path that protesters are marching on to channel them away from hotspots, or aim to gradually split up one very large group into several more manageable ones, shunting one part of the flow of marchers down one street and the next segment down another, etc. Control succeeds the political techniques found in what Foucault calls the "disciplinary societies" (quoted in Deleuze, 1995, p. 177) of the nineteenth to mid-twentieth centuries. In disciplinary societies, people are moved from one enclosed environment to another, in which they learn how to behave as healthy, productive, orderly citizens. The logic of control has transformed and displaced discipline. For example, in control societies we move from conventional schooling in which one receives a credential at the end of an initiatory process (as found in disciplinary societies) to an endless process of life-long learning ("continuing education" (1995, p. 182)), constantly modulating what one needs to learn in relation to ever-changing environments, labour-markets and moving goal-posts.

The disciplinary reference point of objectifying and targeting the capacities of individual bodies is replaced in control societies by "'dividuals,' and masses by "samples, data, markets, or 'banks'" (1995, p. 180). In this regard, individuals are not identified by their signatures or by numbers in mass registries (e.g. the databank of student identification numbers in a university registrar's office). Rather, persons are "dividuated" by the kinds of passwords they hold that regulate and grant access. One finds this shift with the use of a PIN (Personal Identification Number) with bank card products, which have become more fundamental to transactions than the individual using the bankcard. A PIN allows the cardholder to gain access to the digital networks of the banking world and move funds around in cyberspace; this functions to control access to accounts. Financial markets have also undergone substantial changes since currencies (after the abandonment of the post-WWII Bretton-Woods system in 1971) are no longer backed by the gold standard, but are controlled by "floating exchange rates, modulations depending on a code setting sample percentages for various currencies" (1995, p. 180), the US dollar in particular. Economic values are thus subjected to controls rather than to convertibility into units of gold.

In control societies, prison incarceration is becoming supplanted by electronic bracelets for tracking degrees of freedom of movement, thus controlling movement rather than simply confining persons. Deleuze contends that union-based class struggles must also confront this change in type of domination, since historically, the main target of union struggle (the enclosed, supervised space of factory production dependent on the disciplinary type of domination) has moved off-shore. Instead, contemporary unions need to target the mechanisms of control.

Deleuze's "Postscript" and his concept of control societies is arguably his most sociological work, given its attention to apprehending and explaining empirical features of post-war Western societies rather than elaborating a purely philosophical concept. Perhaps, then, control is less a concept and more a function since making a reference to social actuality. It has been productively appropriated in the neo-Foucauldian political sociologies of Nikolas Rose and William Walters. In *Empire* (2000), Michael Hardt and Antonio Negri find in Deleuze's concept a neo-Marxist means to understand the regulatory framework of contemporary global capitalism.

References

Deleuze, Gilles. "Postscript on Control Societies." In *Negotiations*. New York: Columbia University Press, 1995: 177-182.

Hardt, Michael and Antonio Negri. *Empire*. Cambridge, Mass.: Harvard University Press, 2000.

DEMYSTIFYING DELEUZE

Desire

Mickey Vallee

The Deleuzean conception of desire differs radically from those dominated customarily by psychoanalytic and existential philosophy. Deleuze and Guattari formulate their own conception of desire in a manner that is more vitalist than the psychoanalytic paradigm, the latter of which states that desire is born from the lack that an individual experiences as a result of their position in the symbolic order (after they have been required, through social institutions, to revoke their incestuous desire for a bond with the mother and direct this desire elsewhere).

Deleuze's conception of desire first appears in his *Proust and Signs* (2000), which, though made up of the loss and lack for which Proust was famously known, radically challenges the concept. For instance, Deleuze (1996) says of Proust's construction of desire, that "desire for a woman is not so much a desire for the woman as for a landscape, an environment, that is enveloped in this woman" *(L'Abécédaire de Gilles Deleuze)*. Desire is thus the desire to differentiate the self from the current environment and to make a transition towards this new environment, to be enveloped by it. Desire marks first the possibility, and second, the potential for becoming that which one currently is not. The object of desire is a medium into another world, not a world one has lost and is not aware of. For someone like Lacan, desire is the mark of the alienated subject, but for Deleuze, desire is the entry into another world through the medium of the body.

Deleuze and Guattari (2004) are not satisfied with pessimistic models of desire because they establish a tragic end for those attempting to achieve a prescribed identity; that is, according to this model, anyone with desires for objects out of their reach are stigmatized by a conceptual model of transcendence. Their critique aligns with many queer critiques of psychoanalysis that take issue with its pre-ontological condition for achieving the socially sanctioned value of being "healthy" (which coincidentally aligns with the capitalist logic of heterosexual reproduction and family management). Deleuze and Guattari reconceptualize desire in a manner which resists the ideological edifice of psychoanalytic or existential fixations. For Deleuze and Guattari, desire is not born of repression. Desire is the desire for flow.

References

Deleuze, Gilles. *Proust and Signs*. Minneapolis: University of Minnesota Press, 2000.

Deleuze, Gilles and Claire Parnet. "Desire." *L'Abécédaire de Gilles Deleuze.* 1996. Accessed July 18, 2012, < http://www.youtube.com/watch?v=03YWWrKoI5A>.

Deleuze, Gilles and Felix Guattari. *Anti-Oedipus: Capitalism and Schizophrenia*. London: Continuum, 2004.

DEMYSTIFYING DELEUZE

Difference

Charles Manis

A major aspect of Deleuze's *Difference and Repetition* (2004) project is an investigation of the concept of difference, which he pursues through a critique of prior works in the philosophy of difference by thinkers such as Hegel, Leibniz and Nietzsche. Deleuze writes that origins of the "problem" he inherits from these philosophers "lay in confusing the concept of difference with a merely conceptual difference" (p. 30). That is, the problem Deleuze begins with is the degree of willingness of those earlier philosophers to examine difference as it exists within concepts. Deleuze opens the first chapter,

"Difference in Itself," with the object of his search: "Difference is the state in which one can speak of determination as such ... imagine something which distinguishes itself - and yet that from which it distinguishes itself does not distinguish itself from it" (p. 36). His example is a streak of lightning, which stands out from a black sky but to which the black sky clings.

The largest obstacle to a definition of difference as a concept is representation, which renders it unthinkable (Deleuze, 2004, p. 330). The four aspects of representation (and reason) - identity, analogy, opposition and resemblance, each of which have their own failings - block the way by subordinating difference to themselves and mediating difference (pp. 37-38). However, writes Deleuze, "every difference which is not rooted [in representation], is an unbounded, uncoordinated and inorganic difference: too large or too small, not only to be thought but to exist" (p. 330).

Deleuze's lightning-and-sky example proves apt for his endeavor, since an affirmative concept of difference one that does not compare two objects and define difference in the negative – proves elusive. Difference mediated through the aspects of representation remains only a conceptual difference, but we do not arrive at an imaginable unmediated difference.

References

Deleuze, Gilles. *Difference and Repetition*. London: Continuum, 2004.

Duration

Paul Ardoin

Deleuze borrows the term "duration" from turn-of-the-century philosopher Henri Bergson, who first introduced it in his 1889 *Time and Free Will* (2008). Duration is important for Bergson as a way of explaining inner, experienced time, as opposed to the spatialized, clock time we artificially divide into minutes and seconds. Duration is a way of describing our undivided inner flow.

In Deleuze's book on Bergson's thought, *Bergsonism* (1988), Deleuze is particularly interested in duration's ability to "take on or bear all the differences in kind (because it is endowed with the power of qualitatively varying with itself)" (p. 31). Things divided in space "can only ever differ in degree," while something divided temporally (or in duration) is inherently different in kind from other things and its own former selves. At any given moment, our existence in duration means that we are always having a completely new experience. We can never, as Heraclitus tells us, step in the same river twice, and duration is a type of flow.

Duration is, in fact, pure, indivisible, unmeasurable movement, and it is only accessible through an act of what Bergson and Deleuze both call "intuition" (1988, p. 13). This method reveals to us that everything in the universe has its own individual "rhythm of duration, a way of being in time" that is completely unique (p. 32). Uncovering these various durations requires that habit-resisting act of "intuition ... by which we emerge from our own duration" and are finally able to "recognize the existence of other durations" (p. 33).

Perhaps most importantly for Deleuze's own philosophical project, duration manages to be simultaneously "heterogeneous *and* continuous" (1988, p. 37), a unity *and* a multiplicity, a permanent "becoming that endures, a change that is substance itself." We recognize, of course, the centrality in Deleuzian thought of the enduring change that accelerates from the middle.

References

Bergson, Henri. *Time and Free Will: An Essay on the Immediate Data of Consciousness.* New York: Cosimo Books, 2008.

Deleuze, Gilles. *Bergsonism.* Cambridge, Mass.: Zone Books, 1988.

Ecosophy
Jim Morrow

A term developed by Felix Guattari in *The Three Ecologies* (2000). For Guattari, the planet faces imminent catastrophe because humanity has been ignorant of the effects of its "technico-scientific power" (p. 134). Instead of recognizing its limits, humanity adheres to "power formations" that bring about "damage and pollution (pp. 134, 140). In turn, the world is torn apart to fuel "the global marketplace and ... military industrial complexes" (p. 29). However, Guattari is not fatalistic; he asserts, rather, the possibility to remake the world so it may carry on "by a different logic," which he calls "ecosophy" (p. 135).

According to Guattari (2000), ecosophy can reconstitute "social and individual practises" and break the "deathly repetition" of everyday life (p. 133). Ecosophy reinforces the notion that culture is inseparable from nature, meaning that ecology forms the relations between human and non-human - such as animal and vegetable, and incorporeal species, like arts or sciences. Unlike other approaches to ecology - which he views to be reductionist and fixed on Darwinian hierarchies of taxa - ecosophy understands the conditions of modern life to be an effect of relations between "the three ecologies:" social, mental, and environmental:

1. Social: Guattari asserts that all power formations have become decentralized, or in his words, "delocalized" and "deterritorialized," in a manner which deforms established spaces of social and political life (2000, pp. 43, 49, 50). Such a deterritorialization creates "a general equivalence" that "flattens out ... cultural textures of populations," neutralizes public spaces and limits everyday life to consumerist pseudo-participation (p. 65).

2. Mental: The mind is deformed by deterritorialization and environmental damage in a manner similar to the social. The environment has been built so life is marginalized and simplified to benefit "the primacy of infrastructures, structures, or systems" (p. 131). The mind turns into an appendage of "mechanisms of empty repetition;" thought becomes pre-fabricated and ecology littered with "redundancies of images and behaviour" (pp. 27, 61).

3. Environmental: The physical environment is a reflection of a social and mental landscape that is cultivated "like an ornamental garden" (p. 133). Its decimation sustains domesticated, carefully managed forms of life (compare Becoming-animal). As it is deterritorialised, the

ECOSOPHY

environment is walled-off to keep it from growing outside well-planned plots. Its docility gives function to everyday life.

The three ecologies are mutual and reinforcing. Any change in one ecology affects the other two. Likewise, the relations between the ecologies are not fixed; if they can be "reified" in order for power formations to have their way with the world, they can also allow for the "unfolding of animal, vegetable, cosmic, and machinic-becomings" (p. 133).

Guattari called ecosophy "dissensual" (2000, p. 146). It directly confronts contemporary everyday life and its banal mentality by using "our expanded understanding of the whole range of ecological components to set in place new systems of values" (p. 145). And by creating "an environment in the process of being reinvented" (p.68), ecosophy reorganizes the social and mental environment and creates lifestyles that:

1. Subvert "normalized subjectivity" (p. 33). For Guattari, the current disciplinary regulation of everyday life can be remediated by promoting new mediums of self-expression. By altering how the mental and social environments are framed in media and public discourse, as well as relations within the family, ecosophy cultivates different ways of seeing and making the world.

2. Develop practices that modify and reinvent how "we live as couples or in the family, in the urban context or at work, etc." (p. 34). Rather than being organized around serialized behaviors that fixate on ideas of consumption for the sake of consumption or profit - as is the current, unsustainable situation - the social environment must be broadened and "reappropriated by a multitude of new subject-groups" (p. 144). Their purpose, said Guattari, would be to make autonomous modes of "human praxis" and "group being" that allow for self-organization and continuous

reconsideration of personal and political relations (pp. 33, 34).

Guattari compared ecosophy to the work of an artist, valuing the way that art sustains alterity. For him, the work of art is not a reproduction of an existing lifestyle; it is an act of creation that sets up a different way of seeing the world. It gives vitality and expression to the mundane; the work of art creates new, unique ways of being in the world that "spill out across the existing boundaries of the body, the ego, and the individual" (p. 143). Ecosophy, in being like a work of art, is the "catalyst for a gradual reforging and renewal of humanity's confidence in itself starting at the most miniscule level" (p. 68).

References

Guattari, Felix. *The Three Ecologies*. Atlantic Highlands, NJ: Athlone Press, 2000.

Emergence
Robyn Braun

According to Deleuze, "the idea of the possible appears when, instead of grasping each existent in its novelty, the whole of existence is related to a pre-formed element, from which everything is supposed to emerge by simple 'realization'" (1988, p. 20). Emergence is the process by which brand new things come into the world. The intriguing and difficult aspect of this concept is to conceptualize the production of an unprecedented event, something which had previously been beyond our imagination. To help us grasp this difficult idea, Deleuze draws upon his reading of Bergson to distinguish between the idea of the possible and of the virtual (1988).

Bergson argues that the idea of the possible is nothing other than the idea of the real and reality, projected back in time, before it was realized. All of reality then is already completely pre-formed and given, waiting to be discovered. Concepts, ideas and things come into being in a process of selecting out of this pre-formed reality. The possible, then, cannot explain the creation of truly new, unprecedented events, ideas or things (see art and creativity). Not only are we projecting backward our current knowledge and reality, but we are also prevented from grasping the mechanisms of creation.

Emergence is not about accounting for the selection of one possible idea, concept or event, the existence of which has already been determined as possible. Unprecedented events do not emerge from the possible, but from the virtual. Within the virtual can be found bundles of potential functions, beginnings and tendencies. Incipient tendencies and forms develop only to disappear while others arise. When the virtual is actualized, it is forced to differentiate itself from the already real and the possible. Because that which is coming into being is beyond our imagination, and certainly beyond our current knowledge (just like you might say, "it's beyond me how she does it"), the ways in which subject and object come together cannot be determined in advance. Thus emergence is experienced as affective intensity and surprise (see affect).

References

Deleuze, Gilles. *Bergsonism.* Cambridge, Mass.: Zone Books, 1988.

Event

Mickey Vallee

Deleuze's theory of the event first appears in *Difference and Repetition* (a mediator of pure difference between two conceivable worlds), is developed further in *The Logic of Sense* (the *Sense-Event* as the incorporeal interruption of life arising but separate from a proposition), and is revisited in *The Fold* (influenced by Whitehead, referring to the conjoining of infinite forces of intensity). This is not the place to expand on the differences between each definition, but rather to deliver a broad overview elucidating the shared features of event as conceived by Deleuze over his career. It remains the reader's effort to catch those metamorphoses themselves and to create an event of discovery.

The event happens. Its spontaneous occurrence elides our preceding inability to envisage it, even if its determinate mechanisms (forces, affects, circumstances and so forth) have long been in place. At its most obvious, events always contain a trace of the unforeseen - the dawn of the scientific method, the wealth of nations, the French Revolution, Freud's discovery of the unconscious mind, Darwin's publication of *The Origin of Species*, Woodstock, the 9/11 attacks, just to name a few. These events seem to rise above and beyond the conflict with historical social context, yet remain curiously determined by that context's various forces. In a most succinct moment, Deleuze writes:

> Why is every event a kind of plague, war, wound, or death? Is this simply to say that there are more unfortunate than fortunate events? [...] With every event, there is indeed the present moment of its actualization, the moment in which the event is embodied in a state of affairs, an individual, or a person, the moment we designate by saying "*here, the moment has come.*" The future and the past of the event are evaluated only with respect to this definitive present, and from the point of view of that which embodies it. But on the other hand, there is the future and the past of the event considered in itself, sidestepping each present, being free of the limitations of a state of affairs, impersonal and pre-individual, neutral, neither general nor particular, *eventum tantum*. (Deleuze, 2005, p. 172).

EVENT

There is an implausible aspect to the event, an untouchable feature that we try to make clear through our announcements about its arrival. The untouchable aspect is what marks the central feature of the event, namely, *the production of the new*. The new appears in the context of the familiar. The paradox in the event is that what is new can only emerge from within the coordinates of repetitions of the familiar (see difference/repetition). The event is thus not something we can hold onto, but something intangible - a process. So, with the repetition of the familiar, how can the distinguishing feature of the event be the production of the new?

Think, for instance, of the classroom as a potential Event - the classroom determines a series of habits. It is a structure immediately familiar by its design: sit still, organize yourself, turn off your smartphone and conform to your habituated repetition and to every expectation placed on you by every teacher who told you either that you were the best (thereby instilling the impossible representative ideal of yourself to achieve) or that you would never amount to anything (making one comfortable in not reaching for what is new in repetition). How is this situation capable of producing something new if its very atmosphere produces what is familiar?

Central to the event is the idea of the transformation, an ongoing process of life. In the case of the classroom, it remains the choice of the instructor to either facilitate a standard delivery of written notes, or, as Irit Rogoff suggests in "Academy as Potentiality," "to understand this productive disjuncture and its creative possibilities" (2006, p. 13). The production of the new is a discoverable event in the cracks of boredom and similarity produced through the repetition of the familiar.

References

Deleuze, Gilles. *Difference and Repetition.* New York: Columbia University Press, 1994.

Deleuze, Gilles. *The Logic of Sense.* London: Continuum, 2005.

Deleuze, Gilles. *The Fold: Leibniz and the Baroque.* London: Continuum, 2006.

Rogoff, Irit. "Academy as Potentiality", in *Academy*, edited by Angelika Nollert et al., (Frankfurt am Main: Revolver 2006), pp. 13-20.

Fabulation

Jan Jagodzinski

Deleuze draws fabulation from Bergson's essay, *The Two Sources of Morality and Religion* (1963), which refers to a primary instinct that holds a society together through moral obligations. Translated as "myth-making," it points to the animistic forces (spirits and gods) that reinforce social cohesion.

Deleuze and Guattari discuss their particular reworking of Bergson's fabulation in *What is Philosophy?* (1994). It is directly related to their sense of aesthetics as a "visionary faculty" (p. 230). Art's function is to preserve the "being of sensation" monumentally, by which they mean art has to "stand up on its own" (p. 164). "Being of sensation" is preserved as a monument. Monumentalism, however, has nothing to do with memory; rather, a work of art is a "bloc of sensation," which is a "compound of percepts and affects" (p. 164). Percepts are not perceptions and affects are not feelings. Affects are becomings (becoming other, becoming-animal, becoming molecular and so on), while percepts are the structural or diagrammatic aspects of art (see art and creativity, molar/molecular).

According to Deleuze and Guttari, "the monument's action is not memory but fabulation" (1994, pp. 167-8). Hence, Deleuze and Guattari conceptualize fabulation as the vision of percepts and the becoming of affects. The artist is a seer and a becomer. The rendering of sensation as monumental fills the work with non-personal life; that is, with "nonhuman landscapes of nature" and the "nonhuman becomings" of humans. In this way, "percepts can be telescopic or microscopic, giving characters and landscapes giant dimensions as if they were swollen by a life that no lived perception can attain [therefore] all fabulation is the fabulation of giants" (1994, p. 171). monumental fabulated art calls for the invention of future collectivities.

References

Bergson, Henri. *The Two Sources of Morality and Religion.* Notre Dame, Il.: University of Notre Dame Press, 1963.

Deleuze, Gilles and Felix Guattari. *What Is Philosophy?* New York: Columbia University Press, 1994.

Faciality
Carolina Cambre

Deleuze and Guattari foresaw the obsolescence of a hierarchized coding of bodies in which only certain body parts, such as the face, have privilege over other body parts. The rhetoric of faciality is that of a "decoded body." In order to become a "face," one body part has to "overcode" the rest of the body:

> [for] the face is produced only when the head ceases to be a part of the body, when it ceases to be coded by the body, when it ceases to have a multidimensional,

polyvocal corporeal code—when the body, head included, has been decoded and has to be overcoded by something we shall call Face. (Deleuze & Guattari, 1987, p. 170)

Faciality is a code: a construct or convention reflecting how we are used to seeing and interpreting human bodies. This very way of seeing determines how we think about faciality; equally, how we think about faciality is expressed through these ways of seeing.

In related works, Michel Foucault predicted the "end of man" through the trope of the loss of the face (1970, p. 387). Michael Taussig (1999) develops the notion of defacement. Emmanuel Lévinas (1969) theorized the encounter between human beings as taking place with the acceptance of the face, and of the gaze of the other.

References

Deleuze, Gilles and Felix Guattari. *A Thousand Plateaus: Capitalism and Schizophrenia.* Minneapolis: University of Minnesota Press, 1987.

Foucault, Michel. *The Order of Things: An Archaeology of the Human Sciences.* New York: Pantheon Books, 1970.

Taussig, Michael. *Defacement: Public Secrecy and the Labor of the Negative.* Stanford University Press, 1999.

Lévinas, Emmanuel. *Totality and Infinity: An Essay on Exteriority.* Ann Arbor: University of Michigan Press.

Flow
Michael MacDonald

Flow is "an everyday, unqualified notion...It can be a flow of words, a flow of ideas, a flow of shit, a flow of money" (Deleuze, 2004, 219). There are a tremendous variety of flows; flows are material and conceptual (how stories flow from generation to generation), and sometimes both. Flows are fluid (water), economic (capital), material (oil and electricity), commodified (marketing), urban (traffic), social (immigration), waste (sewage), and somatic (blood). In a lecture on Leibniz, Deleuze (1998) wrote about flow, art and philosophy:

> What does a painter create? He creates lines and colors. That suggests that lines and colors are not givens, but are the product of a creation. What is given, quite possibly, one could always call a flow. It's flows that are given, and creation consists in dividing, organizing, connecting flows in such a way that a creation is drawn or made around certain singularities extracted from flows. (p. 78)

Machines in processes of deterritorialization and reterritorialization work upon flows; that is, Deleuze's premise of a world defined by and experienced in motion. Whether it is the physical flow of materiality or the flow of ideas, everything takes a shape, or is, more correctly, becoming-formed. Whether it is the State forming as it works upon flows of history (1983), or the subject-becoming as it works upon flows of desire, all "things" are becoming-things.

References

Deleuze, Gilles. "Vincennes Session of April 15, 1980, Leibniz Seminar." *Discourse: Berkeley journal for theoretical studies in media and culture*, Volume 20, Issue 3 (1998), pp. 77-97.

Deleuze, Gilles. *Desert Islands and Other Texts, 1953-1974.* New York: Semiotext(e), 2004.

Deleuze, Gilles and Felix Guattari. *Anti-Oedipus: Capitalism and Schizophrenia.* Minneapolis: University of Minnesota Press, 1983.

Fold

Michael B. MacDonald

According to Deleuze, "the outside is not a fixed limit but a moving matter animated by peristaltic movements, folds and foldings that together make up an inside: they are not something other than the outside, but precisely the inside of the outside" (1988, pp. 96-7). In a remarkable few pages, Deleuze, through Leibniz, puts Descartes on his head and simultaneously defines interiority (subjectivity) and exteriority (the world) in relation to folds. Descartes' concept of the cogito, which introduced a version of subjectivity, claims that the existence of the objective world relies on the acknowledgment of the subject of itself. Descartes argued that "I think" is actually two simultaneous acts. The first, represented by the I, is the already (mysteriously a priori) acknowledgment of subjectivity before the act of thinking itself. This is reversed in Leibniz and Deleuze:

> I must have a body; it's a moral necessity, a 'requirement.' And in the first place, I must have a body because an obscure object lives in me. But, right from this first argument, Leibniz's originality is tremendous. He is not saying that only the body explains what is obscure in the mind. To the contrary, the mind is obscure, the depths of the mind are dark, and this dark nature is what explains and requires a body. [...] But this first argument gives way to another, which seems to contradict it, and which is even more original. This time, we must have a body because our mind possesses a favored - clear and distinct - zone of expression. (Deleuze, 2006, p. 97)

The fold is fundamental to the entire project of the subject (which began before Deleuze and Descartes) and not separable from it. In Foucault's discussion of the Greeks, the subject emerges from the "relation which force has with itself, a power to affect itself, an affect of self on self" (Deleuze, 1988, p. 101). The subject emerged in Greek thought as a folding of force onto themselves (to dominate others you first must dominate yourself).

The fold is subjectification, but it is also the making of any space. The fold is the act of constructing an interior space in a way that is an extension of the outer, not different from it. Deleuze is able to extend his discussion of becoming, and articulate it in a way that illustrates the mechanics of becoming-subject, becoming-space. The act of becoming has four components (four folds): the material body, relation between forces, knowledge, and the outside world (Deleuze, 1988). One has to be careful here not to fall back to an understanding of being as an expression of an inside-outside binary that brings us back, circuitously, to the Descartes subject-object. The process of folding "comprehends physical, psychological, and cultural phenomena at all levels" (Mullarkey, 1999, p. 101), allowing us to get beyond Descartes to something more like a "wave theory" of the subject and object, which, being as folds, are inter-related and interconnected in the becoming of the world.

References

Deleuze, Gilles. *Foucault.* Minneapolis: University of Minnesota Press, 1988.

Deleuze, Gilles. *The Fold: Leibniz and the Baroque.* London: Continuum, 2006.

Mullarkey, John. "Deleuze and Materialism: One or Several Matters?" In *A Deleuzian Century?* Durham, NC: Duke University Press, 1999: pp. 59-84.

DEMYSTIFYING DELEUZE

Force
Petra Hroch

In Deleuze's ontology, forces are the productive capacities that create the world in its constant change or "becoming." For Deleuze, a force never exists independent of other forces; all of reality, whether chemical, biological, social, economic or political, is the consequence of these interactions: "all phenomena express relations of forces" (Deleuze, 2006, p. 79). As Deleuze writes, "the history of a thing" is the "succession of forces which take possession of it and the co-existence of the forces which struggle for possession" (p. 3). In other words, "things" are not inert, but are:

> a force, [an] expression of force... [every force] is thus essentially related to another force. The being of force is plural, it would be absolutely absurd to think about force in the singular. (2006, p. 6)

In his delineation of the typology of forces, Deleuze describes *active* forces as the dominant forces, those that "command" (2006, p. 40) or "reach out for power" (Nietzsche, quoted in Deleuze, 2006, p. 42), quoted in Deleuze, 2006, p. 42), and *reactive* forces as those that are dominated or that "obey" (2006, p. 40). Deleuze explains how the quantity and quality of a force are related: "forces have quantity, but they also have the quality which corresponds to their difference in quantity: the qualities of force are called 'active' and 'reactive'" (2006, p. 42). Deleuze adds that the "quality" of a force, whether *active* or *reactive,* is "nothing but differences in quantity" - that is, if the quantity of an active force exceeds a reactive force, then the force resulting from that relation will be active, since the active force triumphs over the reactive (or vice versa). However, as he explains, the "difference in quantity" as well as the "respective qualities" of forces in relation originate in the will to power (2006, p. 53). Therefore, although forces are termed "dominant" or "dominating" based on their quantitative difference, there is an underlying quality or tendency in the will to power that determines the quality of the force. Deleuze distinguishes between the qualities of the will to power that, he explains, are "related to the genetic or genealogical element, these fluent, primordial and seminal qualitative elements" and that "must not be confused with the qualities of force" (p. 53). For Deleuze, it is thus crucial to differentiate, as Nietzsche did before him, between the terms *active* and *reactive* when referring to the "original qualities of force," and between *affirmative* and *negative* when referring to the "primordial qualities of the will to power" (pp. 53-54):

> Affirming and denying, appreciating and depreciating, express the will to power just as acting and reacting express force. And just as reactive forces are still forces, the will to deny, nihilism, is still will to power...There is a deep affinity, a complicity, but never a confusion, between action and affirmation, between reaction and negation. (2006, p. 54)

Finally, for Deleuze, as a champion of becoming it is important that affirmation and negation be understood not as mere action and reaction, but rather, as the "immediate qualities of becoming itself;" that is, affirmation must be understood not as action, but as "the power of becoming active," and similarly, negation must be understood not as reaction, but as "a becoming reactive" (p. 54).

References

Deleuze, Gilles. *Nietzsche and Philosophy*. London: Continuum, 2006.

Nietzsche, Friedrich. *Basic Writings of Nietzsche*. New York: Modern Library, 1967.

Surin, Kenneth. "Force". In *Deleuze: Key Concepts*, Edited by Charles J. Stivale. Montreal:

McGill-Queen's University Press, 2011.

DEMYSTIFYING DELEUZE

Haecceities
Matthew Tiessen

According to Deleuze (and Guattari's) ontology, everything that is in the process of becoming (i.e. everything that is) exists as an intersection of forces, affects and processes (of differentiation). We can think, for instance, of ourselves - our desires, drives, movements, decisions, material situation and embodiedness - as a site, a crossing, where forces come into play and intersect. Deleuze and Guattari describe such sites as "haecceities:" a singular set of relations, an individual multiplicity. We are - and everything is - an expression of forces (both knowable and unknowable), a consequence of unpredictable (though determined) affects, relations and determinations. Human beings, then, are not individual subjects at all, but the product of "relations of movement and rest between molecules or particles, capacities to affect and be affected" (Deleuze and Guattari, 1987, p. 261). Deleuze and Guattari warn against an oversimplified view that there exists, on one side, "formed subjects," and on the other, "spatio-temporal coordinates of the haecceity type":

> For you will yield nothing to haecceities unless you realize that that is what you are, and that you are nothing but that. [...] You are longitude and latitude, a set of speeds and slownesses between unformed particles, a set of nonsubjectified affects. You have the individuality of a day, a season, a year, a life (regardless of its duration) a climate, a wind, a fog, a swarm, a pack (regardless of its regularity) ... It should not be thought that a haecceity consists simply of a decor or backdrop that situates subjects, or of appendages that hold things and people to the ground. It is the entire assemblage in its individuated aggregate that is a haecceity; it is this assemblage that is defined by a longitude and a latitude, by speeds and affects, independently of forms and subjects, which belong to another plane. (1987, p. 261)

The artist, for example, exists not as an individual in charge of an environment, but as one component within a haecceity, as one point of intersection in an environment. As Claire Colebrook explains, for Deleuze and Guattari, the subject is never distinct from the environment, but can be distinct from what we might conventionally regard as itself. She notes that not only "can the human be situated in a field of singularities; one can also extend a singularity as human. That is, one can think or develop a singular potential or event in life to the point where human thought extends itself beyond any already constituted image of 'man'" (Colebrook, 2004, p. 1). The nature of these relationships, the bounds of these environments, the trajectories of these affects - of the immanent potentials, the unactualized affordances - are not always apparent. Instead, it is the clichés, the perspectives framed by language and by rigid ways of seeing and knowing, that are most readily observed - sensed - by (as Nietzsche might say) all-too-human humans.

Deleuze and Guattari's description of haecceities recalls Spinoza's pantheism, but without a theistic, God-like being functioning as substance. For them, everything engages machinically in larger and smaller processes of coupling and organization:

> There are only haecceities, affects, subjectless individuations that constitute collective assemblages. Nothing develops, but things arrive late or early, and form this or that assemblage depending on their compositions of speed. Nothing subjectivism, but haecceities form according to compositions of nonsubjectified powers or affects. We call this plane, which knows only longitudes and latitudes, speeds and haecceities, the plane of consistency or composition (as opposed to the plan(e) of organization or development). It is necessarily a plane of immanence and

univocality. We therefore call it the plane of Nature, although nature has nothing to do with it, since on this plane there is no distinction between the natural and the artificial. However many dimensions it may have, it never has a supplementary dimension to that which transpires upon it. That alone makes it natural and immanent. The same goes for the principle of contradiction: this plane could also be called the plane of noncontradiction. The plane of consistency could be called the plane of nonconsistency. (Deleuze and Guattari, 1987, p. 266)

References

Colebrook, Claire. "The Sense of Space: On the Specificity of Affect in Deleuze and Guattari." *Postmodern Culture*, Vol. 15, No. 1 (September 2004): <http://pmc.iath.virginia.edu/issue.904/15.1colebrook.html>, accessed on July 17, 2012

Deleuze, Gilles and Felix Guattari. *A Thousand Plateaus: Capitalism and Schizophrenia*. Minneapolis: University of Minnesota Press, 1987.

Image of Thought

Barret Weber

The image of thought is used to cast light on what Deleuze and Guattari's philosophical works are precisely opposed to. The image of thought can be defined simply as shorthand for dogmatic thought. In terms of the history of philosophy, it is a critique and movement beyond foundational dogmatism of the "I think" in Descartes, a distinction between the cogito (inside) and the world (outside). In *Difference and Repetition*, for example, Deleuze (2004) writes, after describing the theoretical fundamentals of Cartesian philosophy, "We may call this image of thought a dogmatic, orthodox or moral image" (p. 167).

Deleuze defines dogmatic thought as any thought that rests on a philosophical foundation of "common sense" or *doxa* (opinion). This dogmatic foundation can be represented in the simple but universal phrase "everybody thinks," irrespective of the world or culture to which one belongs. In his effort to outline a philosophy of immanence, Deleuze complicates any simple assertion that the origin of all philosophy is in common sense or common being. He uses the image of thought to critique the idea that thought is natural. Thus, he argues in favour of an understanding of philosophy as the quite unnatural procedure of creatively generating concepts from nothing. This, in turn, shows the comparative utility of concepts that have political underpinnings and which push us to think again towards the virtues of creativity.

The image of thought is discussed directly in *Difference and Repetition* (2004) and is revised once again in his last book *What is Philosophy?* (Deleuze and Guattari, 1994). In the first of the two texts, the image of thought is sharply defined in Chapter III as lacking a politics. In *What is Philosophy?*, the image of thought is revised to consider the conditions under which one begins to philosophize. Does philosophy begin in the ebbs and flows of daily life, or does true philosophical thought begin with a *rupture* or encounter with the outside of thought, that is, with non-thought? This appears to be the greatest difference between the two articulations: in *Difference and Repetition*, thought begins with reference to the fact that everyone thinks, whereas in the later work, *What is Philosophy?*, Deleuze would have his readers *think again* about what it means to do philosophy with an eye towards understanding the new and the quest to discover difference.

References

Deleuze, Gilles. *Difference and Repetition*. London: Continuum, 2004.

Deleuze, Gilles and Felix Guattari. *What Is Philosophy?* New York: Columbia University Press, 1994.

DEMYSTIFYING DELEUZE

Immanence / Plane of Immanence

Jason Wallin

In *What is Philosophy?*, Deleuze and Guattari (1994) assert that the plane of immanence is the "ground of philosophy," or rather, that philosophy presupposes a deterritorialized plane as the foundation of its concepts (p. 49). The plane of immanence is hence distinct from transcendent systems of arrangement and ordering.

Immanence is not immanent to some *thing*, but to itself as a movement of pure variation within the thing. Deleuze and Guattari carefully differentiate the plane of immanence from both philosophical concepts and knowledge, referring instead to it as an abstract machine suffusing the concepts that populate it. If concepts are imagined to be "tribal assemblages," Deleuze and Guattari write, then the plane of immanence is the desert body upon which they travel. Put differently, while concepts are intensive concrete assemblages, the plane of immanence is the movement of the infinite, or rather, the flexible milieu required for the experimental elasticity of concepts themselves (p. 36). Rather than being a concept that can be thought, Deleuze and Guattari refer to the plane of immanence as an image of thought, or more complexly, "the image thought gives to itself of what it means to think [about], to make sense *of* thought, to find one's bearings in thought" (p. 37).

Acting as a sieve to chaos, the plane of immanence cannot be represented. Instead, Deleuze and Guattari (1994) write that the ultimate act of philosophy is to show the plane of immanence as a way to think both of the folded non-external outside and non-internal inside of thought, that is, "the unthought within thought" (pp. 59-60). For Deleuze and Guattari, Spinoza's *Ethics* palpates the plane of immanence by "giving infinite speed to thought" - by producing compressions of thought freed from cliché or transcendent overcoding (p. 48). It is in this way that immanence gives us a reason to believe in the powers of this world by constituting a ground for philosophy subtracted from transcendent "programs, design, end, or means" (p. 41). More specifically, the plane of immanence marks an escape from Nietzsche's "four great errors" of philosophical thought: the illusion of transcendence (where immanence is

IMMANENCE / PLANE OF IMMANENCE

thought from the outside as immanent to some thing), the illusion of universals (where the concrete assemblage of the concept is conflated with the plane, and so we are entirely inside philosophy), the illusion of the eternal (where the understanding that concepts must first be created is forgotten), and the illusion of discursiveness (which conflates propositions and concepts in the assumption that everything is a game of words) (p. 50). It is in this way that the plane of immanence founds a way of thinking that is freed from those functionary habits of thought that eschew creation for ready-made ideas and forms.

Deleuze and Guattari (1987) provide a basic pedagogical example of the plane of immanence through reference to origami paper-folding. While origami takes a single piece of paper as its substance, its immanent potential might be expressed through a multiplicity of folds and differential configurations. Though the folded form might appear to have the definitive character of an interior and exterior, these expressions are intimate to the paper's immanent potentials for becoming. What remains unthought herein is the plane of immanence that is presupposed by both "internal" and "external" formations. The plane of immanence hence undercuts the commitment to idealism in Western thought and those binary-machines that capture thought within oppositional or reactive circuits.

At stake is the entire legacy of representational thought, which aspires to material reality to some prior image of how it might be properly formed. By contrast, the infinitely variable plane of immanence is a joyous affirmation of experimentation in lieu of those reactive powers that seek to delimit creation or otherwise obscure the fact that concepts are first created. In *A Thousand Plateaus*, Deleuze and Guattari (1987) write that the plane of immanence is not simply linked to systems of moral judgment, but rather, "allows everything" insofar as it frees and intensifies flows of desiring-production unfettered from both lack and attribution to an individualized subject. The plane of immanence presents events not yet tethered to either the individualized subject or the life of a transcendent Being.

A life is not yet the life of an autobiographical subject or the citizen of democratic idealism. This necessitates a new view of society in which what is common is not rooted in the personal (collectives of individuals, citizens, subjects), but rather, the impersonal (Rajchman, 2000). Immanence presents a fluid "field without subject," possible worlds and conceptual personae freed from the habits of representation (Deleuze and Guattari, 1994, p. 48). Drawing upon the philosophy of Spinoza, Deleuze and Guattari write that "freedom only exists within immanence" (p. 48). That is, immanence allows thought and action to become freed from the stultifying power of the transcendent and the "bad feelings" fulminated by the reduction of creative thought and action coextensive of representational thinking and its obfuscation of the infinite and motile flux in which things might become what they are not yet.

References

Deleuze, Gilles and Felix Guattari. *What Is Philosophy?* New York: Columbia University Press, 1994.

Deleuze, Gilles and Felix Guattari. *A Thousand Plateaus: Capitalism and Schizophrenia.* Minneapolis: University of Minnesota Press, 1987.

Rajchman, John. *The Deleuze Connections.* Cambridge, MA.: MIT Press, 2000.

Imperceptible (Becoming)

Patrick McLane

Becoming-imperceptible is changing with the world such that one begins to pass unnoticed in it. For Deleuze and Guattari, this emphatically does not mean blending in by imitating things. Instead, to become imperceptible is to "make a world" in which one does not stand out (Deleuze and Guattari, 2004, p. 308). They give the example of the Pink Panther cartoon and movies, in which the character of the pink panther "imitates nothing," but can disappear because it "paints the world its color, pink on pink" (p. 12).

Another example of becoming-imperceptible is the way early adopters of cell phones, who once stood out for their rarity, have ceased to be notable because the cell phone is currently ubiquitous. This is a better example than the Pink Panther, which splashes around "its colour" as a sort of signature, insofar as using cell phones was never anyone's personal mark. Deleuze and Guattari insist that one cannot become- imperceptible if tied down to pre-established self-perceptions.

Thus, becoming-imperceptible "requires much asceticism, much sobriety, much creative involution" (p. 308) and much sacrifice. One casts away the things that make one a particular subject in order to join in the world's becoming - or, the same thing, share one's own becoming with the world. Becoming-imperceptible has a positive value in Deleuze's work, because it allows one to resist the selfish majoritarian reproduction of sameness without simply opposing the majority.

Deleuze and Guattari's *A Thousand Plateaus* (2004) is itself an example of becoming-imperceptible. They tell us that in writing their book, they "made use of everything that came within range, what was closest as well as farthest away ... To render imperceptible, not ourselves, but what makes us act, feel, and think" (p. 3). They camouflage their biographies and motivations so as not to be hampered by them. They draw examples from sources ranging from pop culture through to mathematics and the life sciences so as to get in on as much of what is happening in the world as possible. Insofar as our vocabulary is still becoming "Deleuzean" and we often forget how terms like "multiplicity" entered our discussions, Deleuze and Guattari continue becoming-imperceptible.

References

Deleuze, Gilles and Felix Guattari. *A Thousand Plateaus: Capitalism and Schizophrenia.* London: Continuum, 2004.

DEMYSTIFYING DELEUZE

Intensity/ Intensive

Petra Hroch

Intensities produce "everything which happens and everything which appears" (Deleuze, 1994, p. 222). These processes generate more tangible "extensive" properties or qualities (in other words, the tangible properties or qualities of things). Deleuze's focus on intensities is part of an effort to attend to the processes that underlie what we experience as things in the world, which Deleuze calls "extensities." Intensity is "the determinant in the process of actualization" (p. 245).

In *Difference and Repetition*, Deleuze (1994) defines intensity as "an element which is itself difference" and "creates at once both the qualities in the sensible and the transcendent exercise within sensibility" (p. 144). Differences of intensity include differences of level, temperature, pressure, tension and potential, and are, as Deleuze explains, the "sufficient reason of all phenomena, the condition of that which appears" (1994, p. 222). In his emphasis on intensities, Deleuze privileges sensation over form and "invites us to consider affective magnitudes" (Parr, 2008, p. 154). Affect, as Claire Colebrook (2005) underscores, is "*intensive* rather than *extensive*" (p. 38). Whereas extension "organizes the world spatially" into "distributed blocks" that "[differ] only in degree," affect works on us in "divergent ways, differing in kind;" "If we see the world, usually, as a set of extended objects and as part of a uniform and measurable space, this is because we have synthesized intensities" (2005, pp. 38-39). Intensities, Colebrook notes, are not "qualities - such as redness - they are the becoming of qualities: say, the burning and wavering infra-red light that we eventually see *as* red" (p. 39).

In *Intensive Science and Virtual Philosophy*, Manuel DeLanda (2002) differentiates between intensities and extensive properties in textbook thermodynamics: "While two extensive properties [eg. mass or volume] add up in a simple way (two areas add up to a proportionally larger area), intensive properties [eg. pressure, temperature, density] do not add up but rather *average*" (p. 60). DeLanda points to two characteristics of intensities that are crucial to the Deleuzian concept: intensities are "indivisible," meaning that they cannot be divided without changing their nature (a characteristic that is shared by qualities such as colour) but more importantly, intensive properties have a "dynamical aspect" (a characteristic "not shared by qualities"), namely that "differences in thermodynamic intensities are capable of driving a process" (p. 69). In Deleuze's ontology, the crucial role played by intensities is precisely this "productive role which differences play in the driving of fluxes," as well as the capacity to "further *differentiate differences*" in the ongoing, divergently evolving process of becoming (DeLanda, 2002, p. 73.

In *Anti-Oedipus,* Deleuze and Guattari (1983) describe the effect of a state of "zero intensity" in relation to the body without organs as catatonia (p. 329), a state of "total breakdown" in which syntheses are "extinguished completely" - "no connections, no recording, no subject" (Holland, 1999, p. 44). In *A Thousand Plateaus,* Deleuze and Guattari (1987) describe intensities as the driving forces of abstract machines: "Everything escapes, everything creates - never alone, but through an abstract machine that produces continuums of intensity, effects conjunctions of deterritorialization, and extracts expressions and contents" (p. 142).

References

Colebrook, Claire. *Gilles Deleuze.* New York: Routledge, 2005.

DeLanda, Manuel. *Intensive Science and Virtual Philosophy.* London: Continuum, 2002.

Deleuze, Gilles. *Difference and Repetition.* New York: Columbia University Press, 1994.

Deleuze, Gilles and Felix Guattari. *Anti-Oedipus: Capitalism and Schizophrenia.* Minneapolis: University of Minnesota Press, 1983.

Deleuze, Gilles and Felix Guattari. *A Thousand Plateaus: Capitalism and Schizophrenia.* Minneapolis: University of Minnesota Press, 1987.

Holland, Eugene. *Deleuze and Guattari's* Anti-Oedipus*: Introduction to Schizoanalysis.* New York: Routledge, 1999.

Parr, Adrian. *Deleuze and Memorial Culture: Desire, Singular Memory and the Politics of Trauma.* Edinburgh: Edinburgh University Press, 2008.

Line, Line of Flight

Rob Shields

"Lines of Flight" (lignes de fuite, lines of leakage, escape) are used in *A Thousand Plateaus* to describe the moment a process escapes one logic for another order. This also hints at the perspective lines in a classical painting where the "vanishing point" of the lines of perspective is a "pointe de fuite." Imagine spilling water on a table and seeing it run suddenly in one direction towards the lowest point. This describes the experience of the unexpected emergence of an order which defies one's attempts to mop up the puddle of water. As a line, this also has some qualities of a meterological "front" or an invasion that sweeps across an area. In Deleuze and Guattari, "lines" of all kinds are not perimeters but vectors. They do not so much connect as indicate a becoming or direction of flow (Deleuze and Guattari 2004, p.323).

Early in their book, they describe *A Thousand Plateaus* as having articulated segments, strata and areas just like all things, "but also lines of flight, movements of deterritorialization and destratification. The comparative speeds of flow of these lines [of flight] produce phenomena of relative slowness and viscosity, or on the contrary, of precipitation and rupture" ("author's" translation, Deleuze and Guattari 1980, p.3-4; compare Deleuze and Guattari 2004, p.4). Their book is a rhizomatic assemblage, that is, a multiplicity defined only by its limits or edges where it is in contact with other multiplicities or logics. These edges or limits are its "fronts" of expansion or "lines of flight".

Lines of flight are part and parcel of any rhizome, different from more internal "lines of segmentarity" only in their effect of disorganizing a body (see Body without Organs) or stratified assemblage, expanding and thus redefining, rather than stabilizing and defining or stratifying.

Delanda (2002) describes lines of flight as operators that reference the actualization of the potentiality of an assemblage in its context with other assemblages and logics - the puddle in our example expands because it is capable of doing so in the context of a slanted surface. Much later in his book Chaosmos (1995, p.115), Guattari refers to the spiral tracks of subatomic particles as lines of flight.

Finally, Deleuze and Guattari use lines of flight to emphasize the power of experimentation and creativity over the static and stratified.

Thus, for American culture, "the West ... played the role of a line of flight combining travel, hallucination, madness, the Indians, perceptive and mental experimentation, the shifting of frontiers, the rhizome (Ken Kesey and his "fog machine," the beat generation, etc.)" (Deleuze and Guattari 2004, p.520).

References

Deleuze, Gilles et. Felix Guattari. *Capitalisme et Schizophrénie, tome 2: Mille Plateaux*. Paris: Critique, 1980.

Deleuze, Gilles and Felix Guattari. *A Thousand Plateaus: Capitalism and Schizophrenia*. London: Continuum, 2004.

DeLanda, Manuel. *Intensive Science and Virtual Philosophy*. London: Continuum, 2002.

Guattari, Felix. *Chaosmosis: An Ethico-Aesthetic Paradigm*. Bloomington and Indianapolis: Indiana University Press, 1995.

DEMYSTIFYING DELEUZE

Machine
Paul Ardoin

Deleuze's conception of the "machine" allowed him to develop an anti-foundational approach to ethics, time and becoming in order to conceptualize productive processes as immanent. The resurgence of the rationalist materialism of the philosopher Spinoza in France during the 1960s provided a timely foundation for Deleuze to move beyond a reliance on dialectical thinking or transcendental ideas to stress the materiality of modes of relations and their transformations based on immanence. There is, then, no master craftsperson (whether god or human) in charge of production, standing outside of, or above, the process by which things, including people and the built environment, are made.

Deleuze (1983), alongside Guattari, defines "machine" most directly in *Anti-Oedipus*: "A machine may be defined as a *system of interruptions* or breaks" (p. 38). These interruptions and breaks are performed upon a continual flow. One would suspect this makes the flow discontinuous. On the contrary, "the break or interruption conditions this continuity: it presupposes or defines what it cuts into as an ideal continuity" (p. 39). This is because the machine itself is always part of a network of machines, which gives the appearance of starting and stopping flows that are actually continuous and inclusive of the machines themselves:

> In a word, every machine functions as a break in the flow in relation to the machine to which it is connected, but at the same time is also a flow itself, or the production of a flow, in relation to the machine connected to it. (Deleuze and Guattari, 1983, p. 39)

Machines appear to produce starts and stops, but actually just add to a series of and-thens, pre-coded into the larger, abstract flow. When a Kafka character goes in search of a cause or full stop in a bureaucratic machine, he is doomed to fail. All machines - the war machine, the desiring machine, any number of bodily machines, the "*abstract machine* that sweeps them all along" (Deleuze and Guattari, 1987, p. 4) - are flows connected to and interacting with "several different flows" (Deleuze and Guattari, 1983, p. 41). Even a literary work (*A Thousand Plateaus* [1987], for example, or, in the case of *Proust and Signs*

[2000], Proust's *A la Recherche du temps perdu*) is a machine, comparable to a body composed of "cells and vessels" (2000, p. 116) or "plateaus," and able to "waver between several functions" (1983, p. 41) and to connect with several other machines, each of them flows of their own.

References

Deleuze, Gilles. *Proust and Signs.* Minneapolis: University of Minnesota Press, 2000.

Deleuze, Gilles and Felix Guattari. *Anti-Oedipus: Capitalism and Schizophrenia.* Minneapolis: University of Minnesota Press, 1983.

Deleuze, Gilles and Felix Guattari. *A Thousand Plateaus: Capitalism and Schizophrenia.* Minneapolis: University of Minnesota Press, 1987.

DEMYSTIFYING DELEUZE

Machinic Assemblage

Randi Nixon

According to the Deleuzian scholar John Protevi, the term machine "indicates any connection of organs, or a system of flow-breaks" (Protevi, 2009, p. 94). Organs are thus desiring-machines: necessary components of a living body, intimately connected to other organs as they both "take" and "receive" matter-energy that is "siphoned off to flow in the economy of the body" (Protevi, 2009, p. 94). For example, the heart in the body is a machine; its function is reliant on connection to other parts and organs, its vitality is dependent upon the relationships it has with other elements in the system (both internal and external), and it controls the input and output of forces (blood) in the name of the productive whole (for Deleuze and Guattari, the capitalist Oedipal subject-body). Perpetually in "transport" (Massumi, 2002, p. xx) or an act of *becoming*, the machine functions differently depending on the specific assemblage: "passing from one to the other, opening one onto the other, outside any fixed order or determined sequence" (Deleuze and Guattari, 1987, p. 346). How a machine functions depends on how it is connected to other machines and processes.

Machines function specifically within, and are inextricable from, assemblages (Deleuze and Guattari, 1987, p. 457). For example, the book is an assemblage and a "little literary machine" as it harnesses forces (social, economic, semantic and so forth) creates connections between elements and produces its own effects, which are nevertheless connected to other machines, as machines "must be plugged into another machine to work" (p. 4). Deleuze and Guattari stress that any adequate understanding of the social world cannot rely solely on an analysis of the assemblage framework, but must also embark on an exploration of "the age of the machine ... the plane of cosmicizaiton of forces to be harnessed" (p. 343). Thus, attention to historical contexts must be a component of social analysis.

The machinic assemblage derives its composition and capabilities from the specific interactions and exchanges between bodies (moved by actions and passions), that is, how bodies on segmental/machinic axes *affect* and are affected by one another. As Deleuze and Guattari (1987) state, the material/physical aspects of an assemblage relate "not to the production of goods but rather to a precise state of intermingling of bodies in a society, including all the attractions and repulsions, sympathies and antipathies, alterations, amalgamations, penetrations, and expansions that affect bodies of all kinds in their relations to one another" (p. 90). The reference to the Spinozian conception of affect imbues an implicit analysis of power in the analysis of machines: "Each segment is power, a power as well as a figure of desire. Each segment is a machine or a piece of the machine, but the machine cannot be dismantled without each of its contiguous pieces forming a machine in up, taking up more and more place" (Deleuze and Guattari, 1986, 56).

The term "machine" functions to allow Deleuze (and Guattari) to analyze and understand the productive material connections that exist between elements and components that may otherwise be theorized separately, or rely on a problematic subject/object dualism in which the human subject is treated as a transcendent master, rather than itself being dependent upon the same matter and machinic processes as that which s/he is working - the "producer" is also always affected and transformed by the production process, and must be conceptualized in these terms. Taking this idea further, the concept of "machine" opens up the possibility of understanding production without relying on a theory of the subject. In this sense, the machine *is* what it *does* (Colebrook, 2002, pp. 55-56). The machine has no identity, goal, or specific temporal existence, but rather is defined by the specificities of its components. There are sound machines, binary machines, motorized machines, literary machines, human machines and technological machines, all sharing fundamental characteristics. To theorize society/social formations, he opted to start with *machinic processes,* rather than starting with structures like the capitalist mode of production. This allowed Deleuze (like Marx, Gramsci and Althusser) to shift the focus to the synthesizing processes on which capitalism depends (Deleuze and Guattari, 1987, p. 435).

In an interview with Antonio Negri, Deleuze stated that machines do not explain anything in themselves, but instead are components that must be analyzed within the collective arrangement of a particular society. Using the concept of "machines" thus becomes a useful reference point for analyzing the social, not least since, for Deleuze, "each kind of society corresponds to a particular kind of machine" (Deleuze, 1990, p. 175). This has consequences for his conception of historical and social change; it is not so much the world that is changing, but that the organization, structure and components of the machine are shifting.

References

Colebrook, Claire. *Gilles Deleuze.* New York: Routledge, 2002.

Deleuze, Gilles and Felix Guattari. *Kafka: Toward a Minor Literature.* Minneapolis: University of Minnesota Press, 1986.

Deleuze, Gilles and Felix Guattari. *A Thousand Plateaus: Capitalism and Schizophrenia.* Minneapolis: University of Minnesota Press, 1987.

Massumi, Brian. *A Shock to Thought: Expression after Deleuze and Guattari.* London: Routledge, 2002.

Protevi, John. *Political Affect: Connecting the Social and the Somatic.* Minneapolis: University of Minnesota Press, 2009.

Majoritarian/ Minoritarian

Patrick McLane

A majoritarian group is one that sets up an ideal which its members emulate and which they judge everyone else against. This ideal may be quite complex. Deleuze and Guattari (2004) give the example of the "adult-white-heterosexual-European-male-speaking a standard language" (p. 116). A group is majoritarian whenever it violently enforces an ideal, regardless of whether the group's adherents are more or less numerous than members of other groups. By contrast, for

Deleuze and Guattari, any group excluded from identification with the majoritarian ideal is considered minoritarian (2004). As such, the distinction between majoritarian and minoritarian is always relative. A gang might be minoritarian in relation to the general public, but majoritarian in relation to the kids in its neighborhood.

Majoritarianism is problematic because its demands for absolute conformity to the ideal are far too stringent for anybody to live up to. Worse, majoritarianism forbids all creativity. Deleuze and Guattari (2004) write that every becoming will thus necessarily be a becoming-minoritarian and that this provides minoritarian openings to draw majoritarians into their own becomings. For instance, although women may be subsumed as a supporting element within patriarchy, becoming-woman (by continually reinventing what it is to be a woman) disrupts the patriarchal ideal and forces it to adapt.

Deleuze and Guattari apply the majoritarian and minoritarian distinction in thinking about such things as language (2004) and literature (1986) as well. A minor language is the becoming-minoritarian of a major language. It is British English becoming Gaelic English (2004). A minor literature is one which "a minority constructs within a major language" (1986, p. 16), such as the German language work of Franz Kafka, a member of the Jewish minority in Czech-speaking Prague, forever reconfiguring German literature and European culture.

References

Deleuze, Gilles and Felix Guattari. *Kafka: Toward a Minor Literature.* Minneapolis: University of Minnesota Press, 1986.

Deleuze, Gilles and Felix Guattari. *A Thousand Plateaus: Capitalism and Schizophrenia.* London: Continuum, 2004.

Minor

Michael B. MacDonald

The Minor is not a statistical minority necessarily, nor is it a public created by the majority engaged in the politics of establishing "the other." The Minor is creative, affirmative, and becoming-public, whether it is minoritarian or majoritarian. Minor is a flow of difference which has yet to be recognized. For instance, in the early 1970s, one could see Minor in hip hop as a social movement, an "underground" culture developed by artists who used MCing (rapping), DJing, graffiti and break dancing. One can then see the Minor depopulated by a hypothetical statement like, "hip hop is the mainstream popular music industry", and similarly, the hip hop culture as a global social movement.

In *Kafka: Toward a Minor Literature,* Deleuze and Guattari (1986) wrote of Kafka that "a minor literature doesn't come from a minor language; it is rather that which a minority constructs within a major language" (p. 16). The work of the artist, working in the minor, is a double creation. First, it is the work as a work-of-art that stands outside (often outside of many insides), and second, it is art as the social relations of deterritorialization and the territorializing of a people anew:

> It may be that the sound molecules of pop music are at this very moment implanting here and there a people of a new type, singularly indifferent to the orders of the radio, to computer safeguards, to the threat of the atomic bomb. (Deleuze and Guattari, 1987, p. 346)

They suggest that, perhaps, "this can be compared in another context to what blacks in America today are able to do with the English language" (1986, p. 17). The minor is an affective act that creates the possibility of new territories within already existing territories. It is a creative flow of difference within already existing flows.

The Minor has three elements: it is what creatively emerges from a minoritarian means of expression; thus everything becomes political (biopolitical) and "everything takes on a collective value" (1986, p. 17). These three elements create a flow of difference which both negates and affirms simultaneously. The negative function distances the forming Minor from the majority; it is protest. The second is the affirmative creation of a new collective political subjectivity through productive activity (O'Sullivan, 2006, pp. 77-78).

The minor is more often experienced than discussed. It is a special form of productivity Deleuze likes to call "affirmation". It is experienced in establishing the political and socially possible, either in art or in alternative social orders "created by the event" (Deleuze, 2006). The event, seemingly always linked to the Minor, is a flow of articulations territorialized in the creation of affect and difference within space. It was experienced by the generation of Parisian post-structuralists (in which Deleuze places himself) in the events of May '68 - a shocking political act whereby France was effectively shut down by a cascade of events sparked by Parisian university students. But the dream of a possible new world, which led to the protests of May '68, had long since been rendered a political fantasy by the time they wrote *Kafka* in the mid-1970s. By then, their experience of the Minor but had been buried under the stillness and regression of recollection. As Deleuze and Guattari (1986) both learned, the Minor exists within creativity, protest and community-oriented expression, but its enunciation is not ensured: "Minor no longer designates specific literatures but the revolutionary conditions for every literature within the heart of what is called great (or established) literature" (p. 18).

References

Deleuze, Gilles and Felix Guattari. *Kafka: Toward a Minor Literature.* Minneapolis: University of Minnesota Press, 1986.

Deleuze, Gilles and Felix Guattari. *A Thousand Plateaus: Capitalism and Schizophrenia.* Minneapolis: University of Minnesota Press, 1987.

Deleuze, Gilles. *Nietzsche and Philosophy.* London: Continuum, 2006.

O'Sullivan, Simon. *Art Encounters Deleuze and Guattari: Thought Beyond Representation.* Hampshire: Palgrave Macmillan, 2006.

Molar/ Molecular

Robert D. King

Molar and molecular describe an assemblage's (*agencement*) contrasting modes of being, including the various lines, materials and codes that compose it. Yet the two terms always exist "in mixture," and any assemblage will include properties of both. Because any assemblage will include elements of both, one term or the other is chosen when a preponderance of its properties can be located in an assemblage. That preponderance names a tendency of the assemblage, as in "molecular multiplicities" or "molar unities" (Deleuze and Guattari, 2004a).

Molar refers to the distinct edges, surfaces, territories or statistical regularities of assemblages, characterizing them under the various forms of their representation, for instance, as objects might appear to our perception with discrete boundaries. By contrast, molecular refers to the forces that underlie and animate the molar properties of assemblages, including the forces that destabilize them. Molecular forces are also said to undergird actions and events, including the processes through which assemblages come into being (Deleuze and Guattari, 2004a, pp. 300-301). Where molar describes well-constituted, coded wholes or systems, molecular refers to what is open, dynamic, decoding and chaotic in systems. In this sense, the molecular points to processes of a ceaseless, but productive, becoming, whereas molar states through which becoming passes.

Molecularity is thus said of multiplicity, flows and becomings, deterritorializations, rhizomes, haecceities, smooth spaces and minor politics and so forth, while molarity is said of forms of identity and transcendence, striated spaces, subjectifications and majoritarian practices.

While neither term is ontologically privileged in the relation, Deleuze and Guattari align the respective terms to different types of political, artistic, therapeutic or linguistic practice. Thus, for instance, they contrast molecular with molar in order to define a "micropolitics" and a "microphysics of desire," such as can be seen in the tasks they set for schizoanalysis:

> The task of schizoanalysis is that of learning what a subject's desiring-machines are, how they work, with what syntheses, what bursts of energy in the

machine ... with what flows ... what becomings in each case. Moreover, this positive task cannot be separated from indispensible destructions, the destruction of the molar aggregates, the structures and representations that prevent the machine from functioning. (Deleuze and Guattari, 2004b, p. 371)

The therapeutic and political orientations often associated with Deleuze and Guattari must be carefully discerned through a careful negotiation of both the molecular and molar aspects of any assemblage, yet it can often be said, as Eugene Holland has it, that "[t]he aim, in short, is to release molecular desire from the constraints of molar representation" (1999, p. 99).

References

Deleuze, Gilles and Felix Guattari. *A Thousand Plateaus: Capitalism and Schizophrenia.* London: Continuum, 2004a.

Deleuze, Gilles and Felix Guattari. *Anti-Oedipus: Capitalism and Schizophrenia.* London: Continuum, 2004b.

Holland, Eugene. *Deleuze and Guattari's* Anti-Oedipus*: Introduction to Schizoanalysis.* New York: Routledge, 1999.

DEMYSTIFYING DELEUZE

Multiplicity
Patrick McLane

The term multiplicity applies to everything and anything. Deleuze and Guattari use it to stress the fact that all things are composite and that composites are not just the sum of their parts. Talking about multiplicities allows them to mark out distinct assemblages (people, insect swarms, processes, stories or so on) for discussion without getting hung up on whether the assemblage is "essentially" one thing or "basically" many different things. Instead, they understand each multiplicity as a set of elements that may be described equally well as one (set) or multiple (elements) (2004). A group of friends may be considered as an example of a multiplicity. One may describe it as one thing (a group) or as many things - all the friends, their relationships to each other, their collective memories, and so forth. In turn, each friend, relationship and memory is itself a multiplicity, and may be treated as a single thing or as composed of many elements.

Deleuze and Guattari (2004) elaborate on the notion of multiplicity by distinguishing what they call extensive and intensive multiplicities (p. 37). Intensive multiplicities are defined by qualitative changes occurring among their internal relations. By contrast, extensive multiplicities are defined by the relations maintained between each of their elements and a given standard or stereotype.

Returning to the previous example, a group of friends may be understood as an intensive multiplicity. It is easy to understand that changing one relationship in the group changes its whole dynamic. If A and C start dating, for instance, then it is not only the relationship between A and C which changes, but also A and Cs' relationships with B (perhaps A and C have less time for B, or find they get along best with B as a mediator).

The group of friends may also be understood as an extensive multiplicity. What is now important is the relation of each member to a single model, rather than their relations to one another. If the group labels itself as one of Christian biologists adhering to the theory of intelligent design, for instance, membership in that group now depends on sharing those beliefs. If A and C (intelligent design theorists) get involved, the group will still consist of intelligent design theorists, and A, B and C can continue to define themselves as such. On the other hand, if B rejects intelligent design, she is out of the group..Of course, the distinction between intensive and extensive is only conceptual; every multiplicity will be more or less intensive and more or less extensive.

References

Deleuze, Gilles and Felix Guattari. *A Thousand Plateaus: Capitalism and Schizophrenia*. London: Continuum, 2004.

DEMYSTIFYING DELEUZE

Nomadic
Michael B. MacDonald

The nomadic is a concept crucial to the understanding of contemporary decolonization and postcolonial movements. The nomad exists outside of and is uncontained by the laws and customs of the state, a "hunter [that] follows the flows, exhausts them in place, and moves on with them to another place" (Deleuze and Guattari, 2004, p. 162). The nomadic is the conceptual affect that a nomad creates: a relation to the process of deterritorialization. To deterritorialize, the nomad identifies a space of thinking and desiring outside of stratified space, an open thought system that roams outside of codes. As Deleuze and Guattari write, "between the act of producing and the product, something becomes detached, thus giving the vagabond, nomad subject a residuum" (2004, p. 28).

The nomadic is the potential of the nomad, but not to the degree that the latter can fully slip outside of coded space. The act of slipping out of domination, however, is an entry, even in brief, into the nomadic, into "the sense of nomadism as a way of occupying space that is characteristic of nomadic peoples" (Holland, 2004, p. 21). In this sense, the nomadic is "everywhere apparent but remains difficult to conceptualize" (Deleuze and Guattari, 2004a, p. 390). The nomadic prohibits the State from developing into its pure potential, but only to the degree that the former is prohibited by the latter to actualize itself; the nomadic simply chooses the "smooth" space of "vectoral, projective, or topological" (2004a, p. 399) social relations that are opposed to the striations, structures and officially sanctioned orders. Deleuze and Guattari position themselves in *A Thousand Plateaus*, for instance, as nomadic philosophers against a state science that "turns the rest [of nomad science] into a set of strictly limited formulas without any real scientific status" (1987, p. 362). Nomadic space deterritorializes thought, politics, social order and philosophy.

Nomadic groups are most familiar in retrospective forms. Some instances might include the Beats of 1950s America, Hippies in the 1960s, Punks in the 1970s-1980s, culture jammers in the 1990s, and underground hip hop and metal scenes in the contemporary state. The nomadic is not, however, necessarily anti-statist, but it creates a tension within the state: "The State always finds it necessary to repress the nomad and minor sciences ... because they imply a division of labor opposed to the norms of the state" (Deleuze and Guattari, 1987, p. 368).

References

Deleuze, Gilles and Felix Guattari. *A Thousand Plateaus: Capitalism and Schizophrenia.* Minneapolis: University of Minnesota Press, 1987.

Deleuze, Gilles and Felix Guattari. *Anti-Oedipus: Capitalism and Schizophrenia.* London: Continuum, 2004.

Holland, Eugene. "Studies in Applied Nomadology: Jazz Improvisation and Post-Capitalist Markets." In *Deleuze and Music,* edited by Ian Buchanan. Edinburgh: Edinburgh University Press, 2004.

Percepts
Nikhil Jayadevan

A percept is a sensational unit of perception detached from the perceiving individual, revealed most often in art as a heterogeneous combination of parts, or "a compound of percepts and affects" (Deleuze and Guattari, 1994, p. 164, see affect). A percept is different from the lived "perception" of the author who creates a work of art or the audience who perceives it; the percept is central to the independence of art as itself a lived condition, as it has two functions: to make sensation possible for individuals and to contribute towards the self-preservation of art.

How does Ahab see Moby Dick? Is it the simple matter of a sailor seeing a white whale in a blue ocean? How then would we account for his actions? Is his maniacal pursuit of the whale not evidence of him sensing something about that particular whale that forces on him a "becoming-other" to himself, and leads him into non-humanness (see becoming)? The percept is not the brute force of the whale imposing its impression on Ahab, but is rather the ocean itself as something that escapes into virtual existence in the "becoming-whale" of Ahab (and, conversely, the becoming-Ahab of the whale). Ahab is thus a multiplicity - an ever-changing, ever-negotiated whole made by the organization of simplicities. The ocean itself is the zone of indiscernibility into which both Ahab and the whale leak and see the other through. The ocean is an ocean-percept through leaking, where identities become unstable and where singularities become irrational, maimed and monstrous.

The percept is the means by which the perceiver becomes part of the sensation that is both recorded by and preserved in what does the recording - like a jar of pickle-juice. The percept thus allows for the existence itself of the characters and of the work of art because all existence, everything, "is vision, becoming" (Deleuze and Guattari, 1994, p. 169).

The percept is one way art preserves in itself while becoming independent of the artist, the audience, its characters and the materials involved. Indeed, art deterritorializes these four subjects. Even the materials (the paint, the canvas, the marble, the page) that constitute art must "[pass] completely into the sensation," become indiscernible in the sensation, and so become other to themselves (Deleuze and Guattari, 1994, p. 167).

The artistic creation does not mean to serve as an example of a particular worldview. It is not the philosophical concept exemplified or made "physical." Art, instead, is a matter of creating (rather arranging for and preserving) possibles, alternatives to our universe where multiplicities combine in new and alien ways. Just as we imagine that the validation of our existence lies within our universe (if not within us), "sensations, percepts, and affects are beings whose validity lies in themselves" (p. 164). Thus the percept both allows for the characters to feel their way around the plane of composition and to be preserved as art within art.

References

Deleuze, Gilles and Felix Guattari. *What Is Philosophy?* New York: Columbia University Press, 1994.

Plane of Composition

Robert D. King

In their final collaboration, *What is Philosophy?*, Deleuze and Guattari write: "Composition is the sole definition of art. Composition is aesthetic, and what is not composed is not a work of art" (1994, p. 191). The plane of composition is thus a plane of artistic creation, where one creates "compounds" of sensation. Within the act of artistic creation, such compounds of sensation are made up of percepts (like perceptions, but detached from the one who experiences them) and affects (like intensities of feeling without the identifiable states in which they are registered). As Deleuze and Guattari write:

> [s]ensations, percepts, and affects are beings whose validity lies in themselves and exceeds any lived. They could be said to exist in the absence of man because man, as he is caught in stone, on the canvas, or by words, is himself a compound of percepts and affects. (p. 164)

In this sense, Deleuze and Guattari conceive of percepts and affects as "non-human," enacting processes of "becoming-other" and "becoming-animal." It is in this detached, auto-productive sense that works of art are beings of sensation, existing in themselves, without the supports of any given foundation, human or otherwise. A plane of composition, then, is a dynamic field of sensation, an artistic milieu for the construction of percepts and affects. This field or milieu, and the plane of composition which gives it shape, is referred to in *What is Philosophy?* as a "monument" (p. 196).

According to the triadic scheme they develop, "[w]ith its concepts, philosophy brings forth events. Art erects monuments with its sensations. Science constructs states of affairs with its functions" (1994, p. 199). It is on the plane of composition that a monument is erected and "stand[s] up on its own" as a compound or "block" of sensations. Furthermore, "the monument is not something commemorating a past, it is a bloc[k] of present sensations that owe their present sensations only to themselves and that provide the event with the compound that celebrates it" (p. 167).

Still, the plane of composition is not a container or pre-existent space for the act of artistic creation, and so cannot be conceived in terms of any such formal autonomy - it belongs less to the tradition of autonomy than to that of the autopoetics of *What is Philosophy?* The plane of composition belongs neither to the artist, the object nor the artistic medium, but rather to a specifically artistic act or event. For Deleuze and Guattari, the artistic act is preserved in monuments just as the compounds that compose it are created on the plane of composition.

References

Deleuze, Gilles and Felix Guattari. *What Is Philosophy?* New York: Columbia University Press, 1994.

Plane of Consistency

Ronjon Paul Datta

In *A Thousand Plateaus*, "consistency" acts as a concept evolved from Deleuze's intensity as introduced in *Difference and Repetition*, and stands alongside other concepts developed with Guattari such as the Body without Organs, the event, smooth space and so forth. A consistency consists of the power to resist stratification.

A Plane of Consistency (PoC) is the playing field or container of events and relations. It refers to the dimensional character of surfaces (such as a "plane of glass," or "planing a board" to get it smooth and level) on which things connect together in a consistency, resonating with each other in one as a kind of "multiplicity" and thus affecting possibilities for thought and action (Deleuze and Guattari, 1994, p. 19). In this regard, a PoC is also like a "plan," as in a "floor-plan." One can use a floor-plan for thinking through a layout, an arrangement or diagramme of spaces. For example, a floor-plan can help one approach the problem of placing furniture, how people will walk around, use a space and so forth. A PoC is "self-referential: it posits itself and its object at the same time as it is created" (p. 22). So, as in a floor plan, conceptualizing the space that makes it possible to think about where to put the couch does not pre-exist actually having a floor plan. Events (things in the process of becoming something else) happen within a PoC, the dimensions of which can be mapped as the conceptual conditions that made it possible for the event to come into being (see 2004, pp. 290, 294) (for instance, the event of "We ended up putting the couch by the window"). This is why Deleuze and Guattari argued that "the plane of consistency (grid) is the outside of all multiplicities" (2004, p. 10).

Some analogies help in grasping what this concept does for Deleuze. First, "plane" can be understood much as a geometric plane or surface that allows a whole range of lines or figures to be described within the terms of the plane or surface. To take Cartesian geometry, for example, graphing a linear equation helps one to plot, create and describe lines and figures in terms of a two-dimension plane with its two axes (x and y). This is done in terms of pure relations of conceptual elements (a point or a line has no physical area, for example; it is the result of how two axes

PLANE OF CONSISTENCY

are brought into relation by the expression of coordinates). The second term - "consistency" - can be thought of in two ways. First, it reminds us that relations between terms are governed by something like "logical consistency" (that is, "Is an argument internally consistent given its premises? Does it contradict itself or not?"). However, Deleuze invites us to think of consistency in different terms, since thinking about consistency in philosophy (especially logical consistency; cf. 1994, p. 137) has so often meant restricting thinking to systems in which the elements all share a fundamental, underlying identity or commonality ("You can only compare apples with apples," or adding fractions with the same common denominator). The consequence of doing so, as found pre-eminently in Hegel, for instance, is that we end up effacing the creation of differences by focusing on the search for an underlying "sameness" in things. For Deleuze though, "the problem of philosophy is to acquire a consistency without losing the infinite into which thought plunges" (1994, p. 42), which would be the case if the things related are deemed to require a shared underlying common element. Technically then, the "consistency" refers to a relatability determined by a plane and its dimensions, not by some pre-existing commonality. What terms related will have "in common" is a property of the relation, not of the terms. Another way that "consistency" can be thought of follows from the first, as in "To what consistency should I mix this cake batter?" Any "mix" of concepts and elements of thought will have its own kind of consistency. This is where thinking in terms of a PoC meets its close cognate: the plane of immanence (1994, p. 125). Elements, and how they are related, have a consistency immanent to that mix, that is to the pure relatedness of the elements. The PoC thus allows Deleuze to offer a figure of how elements of thought and philosophy are determined and come to be related without being in any way a conventional rationalist. Finally, a PoC is always collective; hence "the construction of the plane is a politics, it necessarily involves a 'collective', collective assemblages, a set of social becomings" (Deleuze and Parnet, 2007, p. 91).

In sum then, the concept of the Plane of Consistency refers to the surface on which elements of thought can come to be related to each other, even if they do not share a pre-existing commonality (or "compatibility" we might say today). A PoC makes it possible for different terms to be related together.

References

Deleuze, Gilles and Claire Parnet. *Dialogues II.* New York: Columbia University Press, 2007.

Deleuze, Gilles and Felix Guattari. *What Is Philosophy?* New York: Columbia University Press, 1994.

Deleuze, Gilles and Felix Guattari. *A Thousand Plateaus: Capitalism and Schizophrenia.* London: Continuum, 2004.

Potential
Petra Hroch

Potential is an affirmative concept meaning the capacity or *power-to* (do something), as opposed to the political sense of having *power-over* (something or someone). As Brian Massumi (2004) explains in his Introduction to *A Thousand Plateaus*, while both *puissance* and *pouvoir* mean "power" in French, for Deleuze, *puissance* denotes a range of potential that he defines as "a 'capacity for existence,' 'a capacity to affect or be affected,' a capacity to multiply connections that may be realized by a given 'body' to varying degrees in different situations" (xviii). *Pouvoir*, meanwhile, denotes "an instituted and reproducible relation of force, a selective concretization of potential" (xviii). Although both types of power are real, potential (*puissance*) relates to what might become, and thus pertains to the virtual, whereas power (*pouvoir*) relates to what is, and thus pertains to the actual (see virtual/actual).

The concept of potential is important to Deleuze's ontology of forces, and to his emphasis on difference and becoming. Not only is the already-actual an expression of prior potentials, but actualization also has underlying potentials that may be expressed in the form of new actualities. Just as actuality unfolds from potentiality, so too do new potentials emerge through differences in the actual: Deleuze writes that the "differential relation" is "the pure element of potentiality" (2004, p. 175).

Following Baruch Spinoza's philosophy of expression and Friedrich Nietzsche's work on the "will to power," Deleuze links potential with the concept of joy. In *L'Abécédaire de Gilles Deleuze*, a dialogue with Claire Parnet (available on YouTube, Deleuze explains that joy is "everything that consists in fulfilling a potential (*remplir une puissance*)," whereas sadness "occurs when one is separated from a potential of which I believed myself, rightly or wrongly, to be capable: I could have done that, but circumstances didn't allow it, or it was forbidden, or etc. – one must say that all sadness is the effect of power (*pouvoir*) over me".

Deleuze's understanding of potential is central to his ethics as well as to his politics. For Deleuze, there are "no bad potentials;" rather, the "bad" resides in "the lowest degree of potential" or power (*pouvoir,* or power over). Thus, he states, "all power is sad, even if those who have it seem to revel in having it, but it is still a sad joy. There are sad joys, and this is a sad joy" (YouTube).

Deleuze defines "wickedness" as "preventing someone from doing what he/she can" or "realizing one's force," all the while underscoring that "there is no bad force, only wicked powers" (YouTube). The political significance of Deleuze's emphasis on potential lies in its reminder that the way things are at present are merely the effects of power, but that potential forces for change are just as real.

References

Deleuze, Gilles. Difference and Repetition. Trans. Paul Patton. New York, NY: Columbia University Press, 2004.

Deleuze, Gilles and Félix Guattari. *Anti-Oedipus: Capitalism and Schizophrenia*. Minneapolis, MN: University of Minnesota Press, 1983.

Deleuze, Gilles and Claire Parnet. "J as in Joy." L'Abécédaire de Gilles Deleuze, avec Claire Parnet. Trans. Ed. Charles J. Stivale. Dir. Pierre-André Boutang, 1996.

Massumi, Brian. "Notes on the Translation and Acknowledgements." In Deleuze, Gilles and Félix Guattari. *A Thousand Plateaus: Capitalism and Schizophrenia*. Trans. Brian Massumi. Minneapolis, MN: University of Minnesota Press, 2004.

DEMYSTIFYING DELEUZE

Power

Ronjon Paul Datta

Power is possessing the ability to execute order, exist, command and create; it can apply to those in positions of power, or those who exercise individual power. For Deleuze, power (in French, "*puissance;*" Latin, "*potentia*") refers to the contingently and relationally constituted capacities (or potentials, both actualized and unactualized) that people have to act and so affect the capacities of others to do things, and in turn, be affected by these relations. There are thus both active and passive dimensions to power. Deleuze asks:

> How does it happen that those who have little stake in power follow, narrowly espouse, or grab for some piece of power? Perhaps it has to do with *investments*, as much economic as unconscious: there exist investments of desire which explain that one can if necessary desire not against one's interests, since interest always follows and appears wherever desire places it, but desire in a way that is deeper and more diffuse than one's interest. (Deleuze quoted in Buchanan, 2008, p. 16)

The question here lodges itself directly at the heart of the Deleuze/Guattarian edifice: the dismantling of binary oppositions and seeing power as a single substance made up of molar and molecular form.

Deleuze's concept refers to an inherently dynamic and relational state of affairs always occurring (or becoming) in socio-historical life. That power is inherently inter-relational means that power relations involve a kind of reciprocity, but one that is asymmetrical because it is shaped by inequalities. In Deleuze's interpretation of Nietzsche, configurations of power relations involve relations of dominance and subordinance between relations of force and their directionality. Quantities (quanta) of forces meet and combine, and so come to dominate other localized relations of force. The resultant contingent combination constitutes the qualities (or properties, we might say) of a body - the differences of quantity (or, inequality) generate a difference of quality.

It is here that Deleuze's reading of Spinoza takes him beyond a Nietzschean focus on what people are actually doing; the issue for Spinoza is about what a body can do. This capacity of what a body can do (and not what it is actually doing right now) is conceptualized as the potential bodies have to affect and be affected, and hence, is broader in its scope of reference. Consequently, any specific, singular body, with localized contingent potentials, does not pre-exist its contingent imbrication in a set of relations of force. Crucially then, individual persons or groups do not possess power because what they are does not pre-exist the contingent relational configuration of the state of affairs one is trying to understand or in which one is trying to intervene. This being the case, the concept of power means resolutely rejecting any essentialism and any instrumentalism about power (power is not something external to persons that they can pick up and use to dominate others). Power thus also makes it possible to transform bodies and capacities, a task to be undertaken by an ethic of experimentation and venturing away from how things are conventionally done. Deleuze's conception of power is closely related to the concepts of desire and machines; in the case of desire, desire refers to how vectors of force relations connect with other force relations (desire adds a dynamic dimension to power). Machines, in turn, channel and divert power and desire.

Reference points and resources upon which Deleuze draws in developing his concept of power include: Bergsonian vitalism; Spinozian materialism; Nietzsche's concepts of will to power, force and relation of domination; and Foucault's concept of power (*pouvoir*). Deleuze and Foucault shared an interest in analyzing how power and desire have been formed and transformed historically, thus giving shape to key features of Western civilization, especially the dangers of the micro-fascism of the self. For both Deleuze and Foucault, intellectuals must attend to the local, contingent formations of power rather than offering universalizing theories. Given their parallel interventions, collegial exchanges and activist solidarity, it is important to nonetheless appreciate a significant and quite massive difference between Deleuze's and Foucault's concepts of power (even while recognizing the significant impact Deleuze's work had on Foucault's conceptualization of power). In contrast to Foucault's concept of power (French, "*pouvoir*") as relations of force actualized in a particular action, power for Deleuze does not only refer to the actualization of actions. Power for Deleuze thus always has virtual and unactualized components that cannot be empirically apprehended. Foucauldian nominalist methodology aims to resolutely guard against any such metaphysics, and in this regard, he remains very much the heir of positivism. As far as similar or largely metatheoretically compatible positions are concerned, the ontology implied by Deleuze's concept of power has affinities with Antonio Negri and with Critical Realism (that is, what is the case does not, and cannot, exhaust what else could actually and possibly be made to be the case).

References

Buchanan, Ian. "Power, Theory and Praxis." In *Deleuze and Politics*, edited by Ian Buchanan and Nicholas Thobum. Edinburgh: Edinburgh University Press, 2004: pp. 13-34.

Refrain
Chris Drohan

Two concepts of refrain must be explained here. The first pertains to a long interview on the history of philosophy and the usefulness of concepts, in which Deleuze listed a number of philosophers who introduced novel concepts in relation to "becoming:" Bergson's "duration," "memory" and "differentiation;" Heidegger's "being;" Derrida's "differance;" and Foucault's "utterance." After the list, the interviewer asks: "And yourselves, do you think you have created any concepts?" To which Deleuze replies: "How about the ritornello? We formulated a concept of the ritornello in philosophy" (2007, p. 385).

First, *ritornello* in the musical sense: In Baroque music, a ritornello is a musical passage that recurs throughout a musical work. In Italian it means, "little return." The french, *ritournelle*, as explained in A Thousand Plateaus, was translated by Brian Massumi as "refrain" (Guattari's later writing on the concept remains faithful to the "ritornello," as found in *The Guattari Reader*).

The second understanding of refrain is found in *A Thousand Plateaus,* where the refrain makes up an entire chapter and is meant to elucidate the process of leaving old territories to create new ones in a continual process of deterritorialization (another word for becoming, see also plane of consistency). A refrain is the act of separating organized territory from material chaos. There are three senses of this act. First, the "rhythm" and "periodic repetition" of the refrain establishes a basic "code" that separates the milieu of the refrain from chaos and creates an organized force in nature with its own purpose. Second, the unique "style" and "quality" of this basic code and rhythm distinguish the milieu of the refrain from all other milieus and organizations, thereby creating a space for it that is separate from all others. Third, the refrain must harmonize with other refrains and milieus such that it finds its own place in the world relative to them, a "territory" from which it can then extended its force throughout the world. A milieu's territory is established precisely when the milieu ceases being merely "functional" (i.e. a force against chaos) and instead becomes "expressive" (i.e. its rhythm harmonizes with others such that they mutually express each other's' distinct place in the world). In this way, the refrain is the first step in creating "art," the act of setting boundaries and making marks upon the world. It is important to note that a refrain need not be sonic but can just as easily be mechanical or visual. For example, just as some birds establish their identity and mark their territory with a sonorous refrain, others achieve the same effect with a particular rhythm of flight or the bright colours of their plumage. Likewise, humans establish territories with a number of different kinds of refrains: songs, flags, slogans, mantras, hand-gestures, dances, uniforms and clothing styles, marches, prayers, currencies, passports, licenses, certificates, jewelry, monuments, artifacts, icons, fences and so on.

References

Deleuze, Gilles. *Two Regimes of Madness: Texts and Interviews 1975-1995*. New York: Semiotext(e), 2007.

Deleuze, Gilles and Felix Guattari. *A Thousand Plateaus: Capitalism and Schizophrenia*. London: Continuum, 2004.

DEMYSTIFYING DELEUZE

Rhizome/ Arborescent

Erin Kruger

Deleuze and Guattari introduce the concept of the rhizome in the opening chapter of *A Thousand Plateaus* as a means to explain a complex "event-structure" that never refers back to a unity or a singular essence. The rhizome is the binding concept of Deleuze and Guattari's edifice as well as the binding concept of *A Thousand Plateaus*, a book which they describe as rhizomatic as an exemplification of their political philosophy. Books, they argue, can be classified into three types: the root-book (classical), the "fascicular root" book (modern) and the rhizome book (their experiment). The first book they describe as the "image of the world-tree," the oldest way of thinking of a book that "imitates the world," a "natural reality," which established binary logic as "the spiritual reality of the root-tree" (2004, p. 5). The second type, the modern book, is one which cuts up objective reality but maintains the unity of the subject who writes it (its author): "The world has lost its pivot; the subject can no longer even dichotimize, but accedes to a higher unity, of ambivalence or over determination, in an always supplementary dimension to that of its object" (p. 7). Meanwhile, a "rhizome" book is "not an image of the world [classical]. It forms a rhizome with the world ..." (p. 12).

Their most elaborate explanation of the rhizome book precedes these distinctions, here truncated for convenience and ease with emphasis on the book as an assemblage:

> A book has neither object nor subject [...]. To attribute the book to a subject is to [...] fabricate a beneficient God to explain geological movements. In a book [...] there are lines of articulation or segmentarity, strata and territories; but there are also lines of flight, movements of deterritorialization and destratification. All this [...] constitutes an *assemblage*. [...] It is a multiplicity [...]. Therefore a book also has no object. As an assemblage, a book has only itself, in connection with other assemblages [...]. We will never ask what a book means, as signified or signifier; we will not look for anything to understand in it. We will ask

RHIZOME/ARBORESCENT

what it functions with [...]. Literature is an assemblage. It has nothing to do with ideology. There is no ideology and never has been (pp. 4-5).

The rhizome is that of true multiplicity that evades categorical representation (2004). Specifically, the rhizome "has no beginning or end, it is always in the middle, between things, interbeing, intermezzo" (p. 27). The rhizome is a model emphasizing a type of thought equated with associations, heterogeneity and multiplicity, and actions characterized by rupture, change, direction and transformation. The metaphor of the rhizome is derived from plants, specifically, the roots of plants as they exist laterally and in dense webs below the surface of the earth. Rather than having one (or many) roots, the rhizome is made entirely of branches of roots, which nest in other branches, forming intertwining and interconnected loops (a rhizome has no "body" at its centre). For Bogard (1998) the rhizome is likened to "neural nets," while Rapaport (1984) compares the concept to a post-Vietnam landscape, "webbed with paddies, bomb craters, villages, jungles, camps, roads and rivers" (p. 137) - what he contends amounts to an evasion of any concrete sense of territory. Writing is an example of how the rhizome can actively dismantle the root-tree. The problem, for Deleuze and Guattari, is that most writing (from any discipline) follows the model of the vertical stem, where everything ultimately returns to traditional, standardized forms of prose. To write rhizomatically, then, requires evaluating each transcription as already several, where each marking is aborescent and internally differentiated (Bogard, 1998). Each concept is already a multiplicity, every book a complex assemblage, a collage of segments and propositions that incorporate lines of flight in the potential for meanings to escape absolute definitions, all the while promoting free expression. Perhaps most importantly, Deleuze and Guattari emphasize that the rhizome should not be considered a static or unitary entity but as movement. The rhizomatic is a "direction" that is always in motion and can be equated with desire in the sense that both "move" and "produce." It is constantly undergoing metamorphosis. Unlike a structure that is defined by a set of points or positions, the rhizome is made of lines and/or contours. As such, it is depicted as an acentered, non-hierarchical and non-signifying series of systems, all of which display themselves in motions and are in constant states of "becoming," growth or evolution.

References

Deleuze, Gilles and Felix Guattari. *A Thousand Plateaus: Capitalism and Schizophrenia.* London: Continuum, 2004.

Bogard, William. "Sense and Segmentarity: Some Markers of a Deleuzeian-Guattarian Sociology." *Sociological Theory,* Vol. 16, No. 1, (March 1998), pp. 52-74.

Schizoanalysis

Mickey Vallee

Before proceeding, it is important to first note that at no time were Deleuze and Guattari romanticizing schizophrenia in their two-volume devotion to the condition, *Capitalism and Schizophrenia*. As an alternative to psychoanalysis, the primary task of schizoanalysis is to overturn psychoanalytic interpretations of desire. Schizoanalysis is not a prescriptive course of action for interrogating flesh-and-blood human beings as much as it positions Deleuze and Guattari's criticism against the inhibiting nature of structuralist and psychoanalytic discourse, which snare the individual in the paradoxes of metonymy, metaphor, substitution, transference, desire and so on. The site of the paradox is the locus of subject-freedom for Deleuze, who claimed in *The Logic of Sense* that while: "[p]aradox is initially that which destroys good sense as the only direction [...] it is also that which destroys common sense as the assignation of fixed identities" (2004, p.5). As the reader will learn elsewhere in this volume, fixed identity is incompatible with Deleuzian philosophy.

Thus, the "schiz" in schizoanalysis comes to mean "to split," to "break down." Schizoanalysis constantly attends to how things always break down in addition to combining and recombining with other things in the process. Schizoanalysis contrasts with psychoanalysis in that the latter aims to put things back together in accordance with the model of the Oedipal triangle.

Schizoanalysis posits that the inner world of the psyche is made up of assemblages of desire that do not necessarily mask a singular definition of being. For Deleuze and Guattari, desire is a constant striving for freedom. Being has no origin prior to experience; there is no primordial substitution, no central subject awaiting the interpreter's deduction. As such, they criticize the principal status of the nuclear family, which they argue is historically constructed through the private sphere of industrialization: the family as the site of reproduction complements and stabilizes the public sphere's site of capitalist production. The stable/repressed neurotic subject of psychoanalysis is ideal for the workforce.

The schizoanalytic stance challenges the mother/father/me trinity by extending the concept of the family into the community and into history, as well as into the assemblages of intensity that gather up throughout someone's lifetime; childhood trauma is indeed still relevant, but not central to the mechanisms of subjectivity. This understanding of self, as constituted by multiple experiences instead of a universal experience, offers relief to the overwhelming guilt and anxiety some human beings suffer over childhood. As Guattari reiterated apart from Deleuze, in schizoanalysis "we have always to deal with ensembles which are either material and/or semiotic, individual and/or collective, actively machine and/or passively fluctuating" (1998, p. 434). He continues:

> [S]chizoanalytical subjectivity is located in the intersection between semiotic flux and machinic flux, in the crossroads between registered perceptions, material and social facts, and especially in the chain of transfomations which ensue from their various modalities of assemblage. (1998, p. 434)

In other words, the subject is formed through a wide variety of interrelated and mutually-shaping moments. Schizoanalysis suggests that experiences at any point in life can provide "feedback" into the assemblages of meaning which interact between unconscious processes and conscious thought, but not in such a way that reduces experience to the prescribed formulation of any analyst.

References

Deleuze, Gilles. *The Logic of Sense*. London: Continuum, 2004. Guattari, Felix. "Schizoanalysis." *The Yale Journal of Criticism*. Vol. 11, No. 2 (1998): pp. 433-439.

DEMYSTIFYING DELEUZE

Sense

John Arthur Sweeney

In Deleuzian terms, sense (sens) is the problematization that occurs when we attempt to articulate what occurs in the complex of concrete experience through language. In *The Logic of Sense*, Deleuze (2004) observes, "It is exactly the boundary between propositions and things" (p. 25). Arguing that any linguistic proposition necessitates denotation, manifestation, and signification, Deleuze argues for a fourth dimension - one beyond representation - that denotes the inherent clash between language and reality. As such, sense is best understood as an event whose locus is becoming - positioning it as the creative process by which meaning gets invested into language, and by extension, reality. As Deleuze intimates, "The splendor and magnificence of the event is sense" (p. 170). The grandeur of sense, then, rests with the power of language to make connections that are virtual but the ramifications of which are decidedly material, as is apparent in the State's recent deployment of "terrorist" as justification for its appropriation of the war machine. It is precisely this productive logic of sense that Deleuze is after, and as the nature of the sense is fundamentally arbitrary, Deleuze contends that sense is simply an effect of nonsense.

Affirming the incorporeal dimension of language as an affect of becoming, and as the effect of the inherent non-sense of reality, Deleuze takes an empirical approach in *The Logic of Sense*, suiting his method to his hypothesis by engaging the work of Lewis Carroll. In using fiction, Deleuze points toward the creative and productive power of language to jettison meaning away from the tyranny of the proposition, which affirms both a normative distribution and/or common sense, and which positions objects in relation to language. This ultimately privileges *being* over *becoming* in its reliance upon a static temporality enacted through a speech act and aimed at making sense of the event across spatial and temporal boundaries.

References

Deleuze, Gilles. *The Logic of Sense*. London: Continuum, 2004.

Smooth Space

Eric S. Jenkins

Smooth space is nomadic space, a space defined by the varying directions of movements rather than boundaries set in place. It is also the space in which the war machine (another Deleuzian concept) develops. The sea and desert, with their vast open expanses, are examples of smooth spaces. The sea serves as a perfect example of this mixing. Originally, the sea presented seafarers with smooth space - a potentially infinite, open space for movement; seafarers guided themselves through a "complex and empirical nomadic system of navigation based on the wind and noise, the colors and sounds of the seas" (Deleuze and Guattari, 1987, p. 479). Eventually, the sea became striated through the plotting of longitude and latitude, and the navigational system changes to an astronomical one. Today, the striated sea, patrolled by state militaries and traversed by traders, coexists with the smooth sea, which still presents the possibilities of open trajectories in continual variance for the individual seafarer, stealthy submarine, or, perhaps, pirate.

Smooth spaces are heterogeneous, demarcated by the multiple trajectories - the path created by something moving through space via force, like a bullet from a gun - of the crossings. Whereas striated space has a defined limit with a top and bottom, smooth space is open and potentially infinite, without definite top, bottom or assigned elements. Weaving creates a striated space, whereas felt constitutes smooth space. Felt is made by rubbing the fibers together, entangling the fibers, creating an aggregate of intrication. It is smooth to the touch, but also heterogeneous, composed of differently entangled elements. Felt is, in principle, potentially infinite, since we could keep entangling more fibers forever, and it has no determined top or bottom, unlike weaving, which requires a secure warp to anchor the mobile woof. The felt is produced by continuous variation - the back and forth, up and down, all-around movements that entangle or intricate, and thereby create the space.

The nomad crossing the desert presents another example. His or her movements are also in continuous variation, thereby constituting smooth space. Thus this space is not sedentary, but marked by what Deleuze and Guattari call "free action" (1987, p. 490). For the nomad, the journey is the thing, not the stops. The lines of trajectory define the space, rather than, as with striated space, the points defining the lines. The nomad might stop at points upon his or her journey, but the points are open, not closed or set in place. In smooth space, the nomad distributes him or herself in the course of his or her movements, according to various speeds and frequencies.

The desert, sea and felt are just a few examples; Deleuze and Guattari also discuss smooth space in games, music and aesthetics. The game GO, where each piece placement creates a new spatial arrangement, represents smooth space. In music, smooth space is constituted by continuous variation, with irregular and undetermined breaks and intervals. The musical form is in continuous unfolding rather than, as with most popular music, set, predetermined and predictable. In aesthetics, smooth space relies upon close-range vision, tactile, or haptic, space and the abstract line. The space is haptic and based upon close-vision because the viewer is a nomad within the image, with every part of the image in constant variation. The point-of-view is not constant but changes according to temporary conditions. Examples here include famous works of nomad art featuring twisted animals without ground beneath them; the animals are not in a set place, their limbs are seen from mobile and varying viewpoints. Other examples are paintings with a constant change in terrain, as if seen by an spinning acrobat, or with limbs pointing in opposite directions from the head that are connected only if the viewer understands them as composed of multiple points of view. Such images are not so much seen as felt, and hence are haptic or affective space. We feel the animal moving, the acrobat flipping, the limbs contorting even though the image does not move and this is not what we see.

Such smooth space also tends towards abstract rather than concrete or organic lines. These lines do not outline the contour of a figure so much as have a trajectory and movement of their own. They constantly vary, delimiting no form and tearing free from the organisms and organization of life, moving like a tornado without regard for set places, limits or determinations. Such lines engage in free action and demarcate the space by their movements.

References

Deleuze, Gilles and Felix Guattari. *A Thousand Plateaus: Capitalism and Schizophrenia*. Minneapolis: University of Minnesota Press, 1987.

Strata

John Arthur Sweeney

Deleuze and Guattari do not analyze culture according to the Saussurean relational model of signifier/signified, whereby a sign is constituted by the arbitrary connection between a sound-image, the signifier (for instance, "cat"), and its mental concept, the signified (the impression of "catness" one perceives). Rather, they prefer to conceptualize culture as the double articulation of content and expression - codified layers of territorialization they call "Strata." The signifier/signified model places culture at the distance of representation, which

Deleuze, throughout all of his work, is philosophically opposed to. Deleuze and Guattari are so radically opposed to binary oppositions that, with the human subject forever theorized at the centre, they construct an elaborate and nearly incomprehensible system of binaries in order to disembowel their hierarchical power. They considered such a hierarchal exercise of constituting the human subject through binary oppositions (straight/gay, clean/dirty, unmarked/marked, us/them and so forth) a facist condition of oppression - a collection of strata that Deleuze and Guattari find strategies to flee from.

But they do not do away with binaries. As the abnormal cannot exist without the normal, strata are born in pairs, and as such, stratum always produce a substratum and appear as "the judgments of God" in their production of borders on otherwise formless topographies (p. 45). In geologic terms, strata are best conceived as layers of rock - matter organized in forms - embedded within the earth - which is why Chapter 3 of *A Thousand Plateaus* is entitled "The Geology of Morals." Their playfulness with binaries is especially prevalent in their detailed discussion of strata. Every stratum (either physico-chemical, organic or anthropomorphic) is made of coded milieus and formed substances - formal Types of organization and substantial Modes of development - and divided into parastrata and epistrata. There are interstatic phenomena between binaries of strata, which itself is divided into transcodings and passages. Strata may be able to serve substrata; their organizational principle is based on an intermingling of rhythm and stratification, but always returns to content and expression. It would be, in our opinion, not worthwhile to "lock in memory the various strata, but rather far better to recognize that it is yet another Deleuze and Guattarian method for composing a vision of subjectivity that privileges movement away from convention, reactions to the State, and which makes it nearly impossible linguistically for any kind of State to rope in a subject. If, as a young scholar, you are unable to lock the subject of your research in their terms, then Deleuze and Guattari have freed the subject from the tyranny of goal-oriented (classificatory bureaucratic) research.

References

Deleuze, Gilles and Felix Guattari. *A Thousand Plateaus: Capitalism and Schizophrenia.* London: Continuum, 2004.

DEMYSTIFYING DELEUZE

Striated Space

Eric S. Jenkins

S triated space stands in opposition to smooth space. It is sedentary space, a space defined by its ordered dimensions like North-South, top-bottom and left-right. The city, with its systems of grids and mappings, is a primary example of striated space. Striated space is opposed point-for-point by smooth space, but Deleuze and Guattari caution that this opposition is only abstract and for analytical purposes, because the two kinds of space exist only in mixture (1987, p.

474) (see virtual/actual). The city, for instance, has ordered (striated) spaces of streets, buildings and addresses, but a child playing within that city's park might carve out their own smooth space as they run here and there. The term striated means "striped," which accounts for the homogeneous grid-like nature of a city designed only to accommodate perpendicular intersections (see, for instance, aerial photographs of Los Angeles). Again, such a conception of a city is only an exercise in abstraction, for the smooth and the striated overlap one another.

Striated spaces typically have discernable limits within which lines are subservient to the points that bind those lines together (with roads and their intersections standing as an adequate example of the line - the road - subordinated to and in service of the point, the intersection). This is why Deleuze and Guattari describe striated space as sedentary space; striation creates spaces to stop and to reside, such as my house on the corner or my city amongst the mass of the country. Thus agriculture is also a favoured example of striated space, both due to its rows and given its connection to the founding of civilization in a stable location, rather than the nomadic movements of people in search of food. With the establishment of a fixed location, a central State apparatus may begin gridding, mapping, plotting and defending its borders. Thus, striated space is also the space of the State apparatus.

Striated space should not exclusively designate global spaces like those of the nation or the city; striated space, like smooth space, can be large or small, global or local, visual or aural, physical or mental. Deleuze and Guattari employ many examples of striated space from games, music, technology, maritime activities and aesthetics. Chess, with its grid and designated movements, is the primary gaming example of striated space. Most popular music constitutes striated space since it relies on an order and succession of distinct patterns intertwining fixed and variable elements. Such music is striated because it organizes horizontal melodic lines and vertical harmonic planes into a fixed, principled, standard distribution of breaks and intervals. In aesthetics, striated space relies on long-distance vision and the constitution of a central perspective to create an optical space. Renaissance or linear perspective landscape paintings establish a single point-of-view for the observer, who gazes into the depths of the painting following the fixed invisible lines that disappear in the background (such as Cartesian perspectivism). This creates a sensation of depth, hence the long-distance aspect of aesthetic striated space. Additionally, this optical space is one for the eye to inhabit and peruse, rather than tactical space - a space for feelings or affects. In this space, lines tend to be concrete not abstract, defining a contour of a represented figure such as a mountain range or a face rather than marking out a varying trajectory that does not necessarily outline a contour or figure.

References

Deleuze, Gilles and Felix Guattari. *A Thousand Plateaus: Capitalism and Schizophrenia.* Minneapolis: University of Minnesota Press, 1987.

Subject
Gregory Kalyniuk

Deleuze's contention with philosophy can be traced to his contention with the cogito, as formulated through Descartes' infamous maxim: "Cogito ergo sum" ("I think hence I exist"). Descartes takes a substantial, completed and well-constituted subject, or cogito, as the precondition for thought, which reduces the link between thought (I think) and being (I exist) to an identifiable instant. Kant introduces to this formulation the category of time, which a passive self receives as the determinable element in which the undetermined I am (or empirical subject) is determined by the I think (or transcendental subject), only to deprive this passive self of all power of synthesis by assuming its sensations to be already formed according to a priori forms of representation (Deleuze, 1994, pp. 85-86).

In opposition to both Descartes and Kant, Deleuze instead proposes to define receptivity in terms of passive syntheses of time, which fracture the determining I and dissolve the determinable self, leaving the formation of larval subjects (conceptions of the subject that are resistant to categorical reduction) - the perpetually aborted outcome of thought experienced as a terrible, difficult and disruptive movement. Turning to Freud, Deleuze likens the passive self to a narcissistic ego and the determining I to a superego: in the absence of its mother, the infant introjects her breast so that it can become identified with its thumb, thus making the lost character of the virtual object (breast) coincide with the disguised character of the real object (thumb) (1994, pp. 110-111).

For Deleuze, however, the introjected object is rather a spatio-temporal dynamism, contracted by the passive synthesis of a larval subject that comes to populate a transcendental field filled with such larval subjects, connected to one another by heterogeneous series that communicate by means of couplings, resonances and forced movements. Borrowing Rimbaud's formulation that I is an Other, Deleuze claims that these centres of envelopment, which make heterogeneous series communicate, belong neither to the I nor to the self, but to the structure of the a priori Other, which nonetheless belongs to the I-Self system as the expression of a possible world (1994, pp. 260-261). In the absence of a Leibnizian God who would choose the most compossible world for windowless monads, the monadic subjects are forced open by the a priori otherness of heterogeneous series running through them, and it is by this process that they are asymmetrically synthesized as nomadic subjects.

References

Deleuze, Gilles. *Difference and Repetition*. New York: Columbia University Press, 1994.

DEMYSTIFYING DELEUZE

Subjectification

Jim Morrow

Subjectification is a term initially introduced by Foucault's discussion of governmentality, and refers to the techniques used by government to create self-regulating individuals complicit with the norms that maintain and reproduce a social structure. The most obvious example of subjectification spans across several agents of socialization, such as the health institutions, education institutions and penal institutions' consistent efforts to compel individuals to become self-governing and disciplined, to care for themselves and, in turn, regulate and govern the actions and interactions of others.

Deleuze and Guattari were fascinated by the very "process" of subjectification beyond the concrete analysis of social institutions. Influenced by Gilbert Simondon's work on "individuation," the concept of process allowed Deleuze and Guattari to re-examine the relation between subject and society, allowing them to discuss the processes of becoming and the body in a way that emphasized potentiality instead of pathology. "The human subject," wrote Guattari in *The Three Ecologies* (2000), "is not a straightforward matter" (p. 131).

In texts he did not co-write with Deleuze, such as *Three Ecologies* and *Chaosophy* (2008), Guattari expanded the idea of process to include "subjectification." To uproot prevailing academic theories of the subject - which he believed to be deterministic and restrictive, reducing life to "intentional transparency" - Guattari wanted to make clear that the subject is "inscribed" through the process of subjectification. The subject, Guattari says, is mediated by the form of the world as much as it is a product of its own function; it is a set of potentials that can unfold in any number of ways, and are only given form in relation to the world around it. Instead of being a static object that exists for itself, Guattari compared the subject to a "terminal" through which multiple processes flow, thereby affecting the development of the subject.

Guattari understood subjectification to be un-Cartesian, as it is not sufficient to think in order "to be." A subject's being-in-the-world precedes cognition, or, to paraphrase Sartre, affect precedes thought, because "a thinking which struggles only to gain a hold on itself merely spins ever more crazily" (2000, p. 131). The subject is, therefore, not given in advance, though it is preceded by an environment that affects its development. Because of subjectification, the subject is an assemblage that is continuously affected and mediated by circumstance and situation.

References

Guattari, Felix. *Chaosophy: Texts and Interviews, 1972-1977.* New York : Semiotext(e), 2008.

Guattari, Felix. *The Three Ecologies.* Atlantic Highlands, NJ: Athlone Press, 2000.

DEMYSTIFYING DELEUZE

Time Image/ Action Image

Jan Jagodzinski

It would require an entirely new set of terms to go through Deleuze's taxonomy of "images" he employs in his extensive philosophical discussion of film. The purpose of this entry is to examine the time image as an example of the central philosophical themes running throughout his work, and to use the action image as a "crisis" point at which, historically, the time image came to dominate modern cinema.

Deleuze's work on cinema is not a philosophical reflection on the meaning of cinema, nor a historical contextualist approach to the cinema. Rather, it is a consideration of how the cinema works philosophically to produce concepts through a variety of images. There are numerous images, but the most important are the time image, belonging to modern cinema, and the movement image, belonging to classical cinema. The movement image consists of perception-image, affect-image and action-image. The time image consists of a new assemblage called "chronosigns," "signs of the order of time, of its internal relations and signs of time as series" (Deleuze, 1989, p. xvi). The movement was affixed to pre-WWII conceptions of subjectivity restricted to the noumenal world and the Cartesian cogito (the thinking subject). The time image is incommensurable and does not rely on "subject." It is grounds for demonstrating the modern philosophy of immanence. Rather than elucidate the basics of these concepts through discussion of film, it is more useful to use Deleuze's work on cinema to explain his philosophy of virtual/actual.

The time image is developed in *Cinema 2: The Time Image* (1989). In a nutshell, the time-image is a direct manifestation of time. Such an image breaks with the movement-image, and its earliest examples are purely optical and sonic (Deleuze calls these opsigns and consigns, respectively). There are also chronosigns where the co-existence of simultaneous time as a series is posited via images. The key or cornerstone time-image is, however, the "crystal image," which is premised on the Bergsonian account that the present is immediately doubled as the virtual and the actual (see

TIME IMAGE/ACTION IMAGE

virtual/actual). Perception is an actual present perception and a virtual memory of the present - the coalescence of virtual and actual time.

The "crystal" is the ongoing splitting and coexistence of the actual and virtual, physical and mental, present and past. The crystal image, therefore, fuses the past tense of the recorded event with the present tense of its viewing. It surpasses the "mirror" as the usual grasp of what perception is as reflection. The crystal image is like a fracture of time, time out-of joint - the moment of looking in the mirror that produces an estrangement, a simultaneous shift in perception where the reflected face appears to emerge out of the mirror as someone else! The actualized face takes a life of its own, which can now be modified over and over - serially. What is actual and what is virtual becomes indiscernible, as in a dream state that has become reality. Bizarrely, movement disappears since the framing of the milieu is no longer evident or cannot be discerned; there is no way of re-presenting the object, no means of differentiating the object and its appearance. It becomes only an image. This becomes possible only when the coordinates of the movement image schema become absent, when the collapse between the object and its reflection occurs - between actor and the role played, between the real and fictional world, between a virtual performance and actual behavior.

The rise of the time-image is attributed to what Deleuze called the crisis of the action-image.

The action-image is the term Deleuze uses for classical Hollywood narrative; it is not directly given in the film but is an impression that arises as "a consequence of the visible [apparent] images themselves and their direct combinations" (Deleuze, 1989, p. 26) in a predictable sequence, depending on the film's genre.

Deleuze develops the concept of the action-image (A-I) in *Cinema 1: The Movement Image* (1986, Chapters 9-10). He incorporates the A-I into his broader idea of the movement image (itself a triangulated assemblage of perception/action/affection). The A-I is, more than any other image developed throughout his two books on cinema, most closely associated with narration, and hence is associated closely with Hollywood cinema (documentary, psycho-social films, western genres and noir and gangster).

Deleuze writes that movie characters are "living images," or centre points, that a configuration of forces impinges upon so as to elicit their actions and reactions. An action-image is a sensori-motor situation whereby objects and settings are given a reality of their own, determined by the poetic or dramatic demands of the situation - a situation which extends into action. The most basic example references the early Lumière films (*Arrival of a Train*, for instance, easily found online and recently re-enacted in the Hollywood film, *Hugo*). In just forty seconds, we have the image of a train (image 1), which conjoins through the movement-images of the train (+image 2, vital image); the action-image is identified whereby it produces an affect causing passengers to move, resulting in a perception-image.

Action-images always encompass the milieu of forces in relation to the action and the reactions of a particular individual or individuals. They are a kind of action-situation or scenario. Deleuze analyzes two forms of the action-image in detail. The first, "the Large Form" action-image, consists of an initial image of a situation (S), wherein there is a "duel" of forces that comprise an Action (A). This leads to a subsequent modification of the Situation (S'). The structure is thus S-A-S', imagined as an hour-glass-shape whereby the first situation (S) funnels and contracts to a central action (A), which then expands out into a second situation (S').

For Deleuze, American westerns, epics and documentaries are full of examples of this large form. An image shows a character in their relation to an actual milieu or situation (S). The character struggles against their fate (A) and changes the situation (S') - intentionally or unintentionally, with intended or unintended consequences. Alternately, caught in a jam (S), the hero finds a way to extricate him or herself (A) and transforms the course of events (S').

The second, "the Small Form" action-image (1986, Chapter 10), has the structure of A-S-A'. Movement begins from an uncertain or equivocal action (A) that clarifies itself (S), which then leads to modified or new action (A'). Deleuze maintained that the self-assurance of the action-image began to fade after WWII and led to the development of the time-image.

An example is where we, as an audience, mistakenly interpret a character's movements to be one thing which are then revealed to be another. In Chaplin's film, *Charlie*, the main character is seen from behind with the movement of his shoulders (A) suggesting he is sobbing, sad about something (S). However, the next shot from the front shows that he is happily shaking a cocktail (A'), producing a visual joke out of the ambiguity of what the audience has seen (shaking shoulders as an indexical sign of sadness).

References

Deleuze, Gilles. *Cinema 1: The Movement Image*. Minneapolis: University of Minnesota Press, 1986.

Deleuze, Gilles. *Cinema 2: The Time Image*. Minneapolis: University of Minnesota Press, 1989.

DEMYSTIFYING DELEUZE

Virtual/
Actual
M. Tiessen

For Deleuze and Guattari, the unknowable and unperceivable dimension of existence is a fundamental contributor to reality insofar as it conditions all actualizations. They call this unactualized dimension of existence the "virtual" realm. They are not alone in offering a theory of this realm (Hegel's offering was the spirit, Freud's the unconscious, Lacan's the Real, Foucault's the episteme, Kristeva the semiotic, and so on). However, while most see this dimension of existence as a determining force responsible for the constriction of our mobility in life, Deleuze and Guattari offer a radical re-reading of it. The virtual, for Deleuze and Guattari, is the unactualized zone of potential that generates the conditions necessary for actualization, which exists in a sort of feedback-loop-relationship with the actual: "the virtual must be defined as strictly a part of the real object - as though the object had one part of itself in the virtual into which it plunged as though into an objective dimension" (Deleuze, 1994, p. 209). Reality is at once virtual and actual. In his guide to Deleuze's *Difference and Repetition,* James Williams describes their overlapping as follows:

> a coconut is both an actual coconut and the intensities or pure becomings it expresses in the encounter with the sensations of individuals (to become hard, to become grainy, to become hairy, to quench, and to nourish). In the actual coconut, there is something of all the other things that can become hard or grainy - that something is their virtual side, the common intensities they express. Importantly, Deleuze deduces the structure of the relations that holds between the virtual and actual side of real things. This structure describes reality as a dynamic relation between the virtual and the actual. (2003, pp. 7-8).

The virtual, then, can be understood as the engine of the actual; additionally, the actual and virtual realms can be thought of as responding to one another in a conversation between problem and solution, such that the virtual realm responds to and creates the problems that define the actual (and vice versa). Deleuze and Guattari explain that the virtual "possesses the reality of a task to be performed or a problem to be solved: it is the problem which orientates, conditions, and engenders solutions," but add that these solutions do "not resemble the conditions of the problem" (Deleuze, 1994, p. 212).

For Deleuze and Guattari, then, unknowable virtual forces generate or make possible both the problems and the solutions that compose everyday life. Moreover, the virtual dimension of existence can be thought to exceed the actual one insofar as it is a realm of pure potential that need not correspond to any particular situation, entity or set of circumstances, since, as pure potential, it is always in the process of, literally, exceeding and differentiating itself from the discrete sets of possibles that have just now been actualized:

> The only danger in all this is that the virtual could be confused with the possible. The possible is opposed to the real; the process undergone by the possible is therefore a 'realisation.' By contrast, the virtual is not opposed to the real; it possesses a full reality by itself. The process it undergoes is that of actualization. It would be wrong to see only a verbal dispute here: it is a question of existence itself. (Deleuze, 1994, p. 211)

That is, as far as Deleuze and Guattari are concerned, virtualities - as potential - are never exhausted. Indeed, most of them never contribute to anything actual, always exceeding those potentials that are actualized, occupying a space immanent to but distinct from the actual world. Deleuze describes the virtual as a realm of pure creativity, as an engine of production, as the inexhaustible fount into which the actual plunges (1994, p. 209) in order to extract its solutions to its problems.

The virtual dimension does not exceed the actual dimension; rather, the former is adequate to the latter's requirement to remain an actual dimension, impregnating it with all the excessive virtualities it will ever need. The actual is not itself excessive, but is composed of excessive virtual qualities. In other words, for the actual realm to manifest the change required to maintain a dynamic over time, the virtual realm of potential must be capable of serving up a multiplicity of potential options for said change, a multiplicity that inevitably exceeds any particular actualization.

According to this logic, the actual is never excessive, since actualizations are determinations from the direction of the virtual - actualizations are solutions to the variety of problems posed by virtual excess. Excess, then, is not an appropriate ontological category for thinking about the actual (whether the actual we are thinking about is breakfast or a painting). If we follow Deleuze, however, excess might be a useful category to help us think about change and potential that comes from the virtual through the actual. As such, a given thing's virtual dimension could be said to be excessive insofar as the virtual dimension of being exists as an uncountable field of inexhaustibly creative potential.

It is important to recognize that the virtual - while manifesting excessive potentials - is granted these potentials by the anchoring conditions of the actual. Deleuze explains:

> The reality of the virtual consists of the differential elements and relations along with the singular points which

> correspond to them. The reality of the virtual is structure. We must avoid giving the elements and relations which form a structure an actuality which they do not have, and withdrawing from them a reality which they have. We have seen that a double process of reciprocal determination and complete determination defined that reality: far from being undetermined, the virtual is completely determined. When it is claimed that works of art are immersed in a virtuality, what is being invoked is not some confused determination but the completely determined structure formed by its genetic differential elements, its 'virtual' or 'embryonic' elements. The elements, varieties of relations and singular points coexist in the work or the object, in the virtual part of the work or object, without it being possible to designate a point of view privileged over others, a centre which would unify the other centres. [...] What the complete determination lacks is the whole set of relations belonging to actual existence. (Deleuze, 1994, p. 209)

In other words, the reciprocal determinations produced by the virtual and actual realms are not so much excessive as they are necessary; "everything is necessary, either from its essence or from its cause: Necessity is the only affection of Being, the only modality" (Deleuze, 1990, p. 38-9). Deleuze's ontology, then, is premised upon virtuality's relative excessiveness preceding and determining all expressions of actuality. For him, it is thanks to virtuality's excessiveness that entities have the potential to be, to make and to become an effectively infinite - though determined - number of things (in accordance with their capacities).

References

Deleuze, Gilles. *Difference and Repetition.* New York: Columbia University Press, 1994.

Deleuze, Gilles. *Expressionism in Philosophy: Spinoza.* Cambridge, Mass.: MIT Press, 1990.

Williams, James. *Gilles Deleuze's* Difference and Repetition: *A Critical Introduction and Guide.* Edinburgh: Edinburgh University Press, 2003.

War Machine

Eric Jenkins

When the Occupy Protests of 2011 descended on Wall Street and similar places in cities around the world, was there anything more striking about their assembly than their lack of centralized leadership? They did not fight against a specific social injustice, but rather, against an entire system that subjectivized them as individuals without the agency to transcend their class status. Indeed, the demand made by the State for them to *have* demands was an exercise of State power. As Judith Butler noted in her observations of Occupy, "to appeal to that authority [of the State] to satisfy the demand would be one way of attributing legitimacy to that authority" (2012, p. 10). Here, we can read the international Occupy movement as a "war machine," armed not with militaristic weaponry, but an assemblage of forces launched against the very form of State power.

Deleuze and Guattari conceive of the "war machine" in their "Treatise on Nomadology" (Chapter 12, *A Thousand Plateaus*). The war machine is a social apparatus or a dispotif, to borrow a term from Foucault, an interactive assemblage of forces that produce specific power/knowledge formations through discourse. The war machine is a form of expression of a nomadic way of becoming. The war machine is not complicit with the State apparatus of militaristic conquest; it is a concept which expresses the opposition to convention and to the State. The nomad is equally important in this conception as an assemblage which radically opposes the State and in which lurks the possibility of the new - a new social order, a new way of feeling, thinking, new assembly, and so forth.

The nomadic war machine is external to and opposes both the State apparatus and the primitive city-state: "it is determined in such a way as to destroy the State-form and the city-form with which it collides" (Deleuze and Guattari, 1987, p. 418). Two primary examples include Genghis Khan and Moses. As the Israelites fled Egypt and wandered the smooth space of the desert, they encountered cities and States blocking their line of flight. This resulted in war. Nomads like Khan and Moses seek a line of flight, creating smooth space via their trajectories. These trajectories, however, clash with the striated space of the State apparatus. Battles result. Thus such packs or bands of nomads must organize to protect themselves and enforce their line of flight. The war machine is the resultant apparatus.

The concept of the war machine counters many evolutionary accounts of history that consider nomads as primitive and disorganized, not evolved enough to form a State. Deleuze and Guattari, in contrast, see the war machine as a highly organized and complex social apparatus. The war machine attempts to prevent the rise of a State, a centralization of power, a striation of space. They actively deny the rise of a king or political system through complex inhibiting mechanisms that distribute power. These micromechanisms are similar to the unwritten dynamic codes of such groups as gangs or packs. Hence, the war machine is always a becoming-animal, a social organization adopting the tactics of banding animals. One seemingly human characteristic of these war machines is their distribution of power numerically, rather than lineally or territorially. Primitive tribes distribute power through lineage; the king begets a prince, for instance. The State apparatus distributes power territorially, by assigning land and creating control over that land. The war machine, however, distributes power numerically, in order to prevent the rise of a town or a State. The bands of nomads are assigned numbers, preventing lineage from being the organizing principle (though for a special group, Moses and the Hebrews, the first born of each tribe was selected and numbered - a sort of check on the centralization of power in the leader).

The war machine may sound like its purpose is to create war. This is only true in some instances, namely when it is appropriated by the State. The State does not have its own war machine; it works through other agencies, such as the police and the prisons (what Althusser called the "Ideological State Apparatuses," or Foucault, the "technologies of power"). Yet the State often finds itself drawn into war, either with nomads or other states. Thus they appropriate the war machine, turning it into an armed force, organized in many different ways across history (sometimes a mercenary army, sometimes professional). When the State appropriates the war machine, it gives the machine the goal of either creating war or maintaining what Deleuze and Guattari call the "peace of Terror" (1987, p. 421). Only then does war become the proper object or purpose of the war machine. When under nomadic direction, the war machine's purpose is not necessarily to fight war. Sometimes, the war machine helps avoid battles; at other times, it stages them. Yet war always accompanies the war machine because in carving a line of flight in smooth space, the nomad inevitably encounters and clashes with the city and the State.

Reference

Deleuze, Gilles and Felix Guattari. *A Thousand Plateaus: Capitalism and Schizophrenia.* Minneapolis: University of Minnesota Press, 1987.

Butler, Judith. "So, What Are The Demands? And Where Do They Go From Here?" *Tidal: Occupy Theory, Occupy Strategy,* Issue 2, March 2012: pp. 8-11.

Contributors

Paul Ardoin (Florida State University) is the co-editor of *Understanding Bergson, Understanding Modernism* (forthcoming, Continuum). His work has appeared or is forthcoming in *Philosophy and Literature, Transnational Literature*, and *LIT: Literature, Interpretation, Theory*. His recent research focuses on Deleuze's readings of Samuel Beckett.

Robyn Braun is Assistant Professor in the Department of Sociology and the Science, Technology and Society program at the University of Alberta. Her research interests include social studies of science and knowledge, historical epistemology, histories and theories of biopolitics and the philosophies of Georges Canguihem, Michel Foucault and Giles Deleuze. She is currently finishing a manuscript on the history of vitamins and looking ahead to histories of marine mammal science.

Carolina Cambre teaches in the Sociology department at King's University College at Western University Ontario. Her interests focus on critical policy analysis, and the issue of representation through semiotics, contemporary social theory, and with respect to the literature in visual cultural studies, communication and discourse analysis. As an artist she also embraces artistic approaches to research and activism in the area of social justice.

Ronjon Paul Datta is Assistant Professor of Social Theory and Cultural Studies and Director of the Intermedia Research Studio in the Department of Sociology at the University of Alberta. He specializes in contemporary and classical social theory, political sociology, metatheory and the sociology of the sacred.

Christopher M Drohan is currently an Assistant Director at the European Graduate School of Media and Communication, Saas-Fee, Switzerland. He earned his PhD, on the semiotics of Gilles Deleuze, in 2007 from EGS. Drohan is also Chief Editor of *Semiophagy: Journal of Pataphysics and Existential Semiotics* (www.semiophagy.com). Recently, he has published several articles on global semiotics, philosophy in graphic novels, and the phenomenology of travel.

Petra Hroch is a PhD Candidate, SSHRC Canada Graduate Scholar, and Izaak Walton Killam Memorial Scholar in Theory & Culture in the Department of Sociology at the University of Alberta. Her research interests include art & design, aesthetics and politics, and contemporary critical, social, and cultural theory. Her dissertation focuses on new materialist and posthumanist theory, environmental sustainability, and sustainable design philosophies and practices. Petra's work appears in *Walter Benjamin and the Aesthetics of Change* (Palgrave 2010), *Ecologies of Affect: Placing Nostalgia, Desire and Hope* (Wilfrid Laurier University Press 2011) and the forthcoming *For a people-yet-to-come: Deleuze, Politics, and Education* (Continuum).

Jan Jagodzinski is a Professor in the Department of Secondary Education, University of Alberta in Edmonton, Alberta, Canada. His most recent edited book is *Psychoanalyzing Cinema: A Productive Encounter with Lacan, Deleuze and Žižek* (Palgrave, 2012).

Eric S. Jenkins is an assistant professor of communication at the University of Cincinnati. His research concerns the relationship between media and consumerism. He has published articles in *Critical Inquiry*, *Critical Studies in Media Communication*, *Quarterly Journal of Film and Video*, and *Explorations in Media Ecology*.

Nikhil Jayadevan is an MA student in the English Department at the University of Alberta. He is interested mainly in theoretical takes on humour, seriousness, and the State. He enjoys writing fiction and stand-up material and hates taking long walks.

Gregory Kalyniuk is completing his Ph.D. in Cultural Studies at Trent University in Peterborough, Canada, where he has taught seminars on Modern Culture and Science Fiction, and currently teaches a course on Civilisation and Human Nature. His background is in Philosophy and Social and Cultural Anthropology. His Ph.D. dissertation, entitled *Individuation, Intensity, and Humour in Deleuze's Philosophy*, elucidates Deleuze's theory of humour by connecting its different instances while extrapolating upon some of its loose ends.

Robert D. King is by training a student of European, Continental philosophy and a strong admirer of Hegel's Science of Logic. He regularly teaches courses in history, philosophy, literary criticism, and world civilizations

CONTRIBUTORS

Erin Kruger primarily researches at the University of Western Sydney in law and society, and science and technology studies, with a wide range of research interests including forensic science, criminal law, evidence, history and philosophy of science, social theory, and cultural theory. Her current research, entitled 'Between Science and Law', challenges the predominant view of criminal law and forensic science as separate disciplines by considering the interconnected nature of these relations through the often stabilizing, but equally contingent, nature of visual evidence.

Bradley Lafortune holds a Masters in English Literature from the University of Alberta, and will likely be a lifelong reader of Gilles Deleuze's philosophy. During his time as an immiserated and exuberant graduate student, Bradley found joy and frustration in reading Deleuze with fellow enthusiasts and detractors, especially in the context of emancipatory political economy. Currently, he is trying to embrace the non-fascist life.

Michael B. MacDonald is a sociomusicologist or popular music ethnomusicologist researching cultural sustainability within the emergence of the creative economy. Michael currently teaches popular music courses at the University of Alberta and is a creative economy researcher with Creative Alberta.

Charles Manis lives in Philadelphia, PA, and is currently pursuing his PhD in English Literature at Temple University. He received his MFA in Creative Writing from Florida State University. His work is forthcoming or has recently appeared in *Transnational Literature, Fifth Wednesday*, and *RATTLE*.

Patrick McLane is Doctoral Candidate in Sociology at the University of Alberta. He studies socio-legal studies and sovereignty politics.

James Morrow is a researcher at Katholische Universität Eichstätt-Ingolstadt. He is also editor of Risk & Consequence.

Randi Nixon is a PhD student in Sociology at the University of Alberta. Her interests include Deleuzian/Spinozan renderings of affect, feminist and queer politics, and the interconnectedness of body politics and political bodies, particularly in political mobilizations of pride.

John A. Sweeney is a PhD candidate in the Department of Political Science at the University of

Hawaii at Manoa focusing on Futures Studies, Political Theory, and Cultural Studies. John's dissertation looks at the nexus of affect between the unhuman and human using speculative, material, and aesthetic frames. He still isn't much of a surfer but hopes to stick around the islands long enough to get decent

Matthew Tiessen is a SSHRC Postdoctoral Research Fellow at the Infoscape Research Lab in the Faculty of Communication and Design at Ryerson University. He teaches and publishes in the area of technology studies, digital culture, and visual culture. His research has been featured in such publications as: *Theory, Culture & Society*; *Volume*; *CTheory*; *Rhizomes: Cultural Studies in Emerging Knowledge*; *Surveillance & Society*; *Space and Culture*; *Pli: The Warwick Journal of Philosophy*; *Revisiting Normativity with Deleuze* (2012, Continuum); *Ecologies of Affect: Placing Nostalgia, Desire, and Hope* (2010, Wilfrid Laurier University Press); and *What Is a City? Rethinking the Urban after Hurricane Katrina* (2008, University of Georgia Press). He is also an exhibiting artist.

Jason J. Wallin is Assistant Professor of Media and Youth Culture in Curriculum in the Faculty of Education at the University of Alberta, Canada, where he teaches courses in visual art, media studies, and cultural curriculum theory. He is the author of *A Deleuzian Approach to Curriculum: Essays on a Pedagogical Life* (Palgrave Macmillan), co-author of the forthcoming *Arts-Based Research: A Critique and Proposal* (with jan jagodzinski, Sense Publishers), and co-editor of the forthcoming collection *Deleuze, Guattari, Politics and Education* (with Matt Carlin, Continuum).

Barret Weber teaches social theory in Sociology at the University of Alberta. He has just produced a PhD thesis on the Inuit of the Canadian north and the creation of Nunavut. His future research will focus on Arctic urbanization and the political theory of hunter gatherers and settlers in Canada.

www.ingramcontent.com/pod-product-compliance
Lightning Source LLC
Chambersburg PA
CBHW051053160426
43193CB00010B/1175